T0247329

PENGUIN BOOKS

AND FOR THE RECORD

Yugel Losorata is a journalist-musician, born and raised in the Philippines.

Since the year 2000 he has written articles touching various subjects in the fields of entertainment, arts, lifestyle, business, and sports. He has also been composing and recording songs released in the form of physical and digital albums, EPs, and singles. He co-founded two bands, Syato and The Pub Forties, where he served as chief songwriter, co-singer, and bass player for twenty years combined. He also wrote for and collaborated with other artists.

Losorata's byline has appeared in various Philippine publications with nationwide circulation, including *Manila Bulletin*, *The Philippine Star*, and *Manila Standard* where he has been writing a weekly column. Online, he has contributions uploaded on *Yahoo Philippines* (Southeast Asia), and *Philippine Entertainment Portal (PEP.ph)*. He also worked as staff writer at *Manila Bulletin* and as a senior copy editor at *CNN Philippines*.

As an author he wrote four books at the height of the pandemic. In 2020 he penned *How to Survive the New Normal* and *30 Midnights of Flash Fiction*. In 2021, his novel *The Lust Regime* and a collection of short stories, *Rhythm & Bruise*, were published, with the latter featuring a foreword by the Philippines' 'King of Talk' Boy Abunda.

The family man is currently residing in the United States of America.

ADVANCE PRAISE FOR *AND FOR THE RECORD*

'Yugel's frank, vivid, and endearing memoir has reaffirmed why I love being a musician—the challenges and fulfilments that come with being one. It also upheld my commitment to my art with a renewed conviction to seek new adventures and surprises not unlike his own journey. And it made me more grateful for having been bestowed the ability to play with one of the most magical of life's gifts: music.'

—Medwin Marfil
Lead vocalist and chief songwriter
of Filipino band True Faith

'Yugel's book embodies the spirit of innovation and cultural pride that inspires, provokes thought, and evokes emotions. As Filipino musicians carve out their place in the rich tapestry of music history, these bands and their music are poised to leave an indelible imprint on the hearts and minds of listeners.'

—Rico Hizon
Former news anchor of *CNBC Business News*,
BBC World News, and *CNN Philippines*

'Let Yugel Losorata hold your hand in a guided tour of the Philippine music scene in this book chronicling the highs and lows of his years as a music journalist and band player-composer. What a rare, smashing combination!

This book makes for an easy listening to music lovers, and not just for fans who love to rock and swear to roll.'

—Nestor Cuartero
Entertainment journalist,
book author, and journalism lecturer

'Yugel, the man I am honoured to call "my best friend", emanates brilliance and pure talent. He can take his everyday experiences and craftily deconstruct and construct it into messages that are beautiful, significant and impactful to every age and generation.
In his new book, you will get a peek into his insights and tenacity. Hopefully this inspires and moves you in such a way that he has inspired and moved me to face my own challenges, pursue my vision, and live my dreams.'

—Ronald 'Joaqui' Tupas
US-based Filipino actor,
commercial model, and vlogger

'Yugel Losorata sets the record straight on what has been an eventful career in music, both as a musician and as a journalist covering the scene.

Yugel's invaluable insights and often candid approach in sharing his own story makes this book a must-read for everyone who loves music, especially those who hope to build a lasting career in this particular field.'

—Edwin Sallan
Music journalist, soundstrip
editor for *Business Mirror*

'Yugel has the three P's desirable in every project. He is most patient, positive, and persistent. He never lets go of his vision as he hopes for people to show up in his life at the right time. I believe I had the privilege to be one of those who fitted into Yugel's projects at the right place and hour. Through his band and music, I got my playing and art on Spotify.'

—Jeanette Kamphuis
Violinist and visual artist

'I am so pleased that Yugel has come up with this precious memoir of his.'

—Ogie Alcasid
Singer-songwriter, comedian, actor

'Words and music have been the allies of Yugel in his colourful journey. He knows the music biz by heart, and it shows. His book is sort of an exposé of his love affair with lyrics, melodies and the written word. He candidly shares what it's like to be on centre stage as a musician and backstage as a music journalist. Talk about having the best of both worlds.

Yugel's stories will inspire you to keep the music playing even when things have gone off-key. *And for the Record* is like a tune that leads to a 'last song syndrome.' The author's words linger on.

—Dolly Anne Carvajal
Showbiz columnist, *Philippine Daily Inquirer*

'I always love a story about humble beginnings, taking a leap of faith without regrets, and surfacing above these challenges as one's own victor—that is how Yugel Losorata's *And for the Record* resonated to me. I can identify with the author's journey as an artist and as a passionate risk-taker in life, as poignantly narrated in the vignettes chronicling his career. These imbued strong emotions, most especially empathy.

This book is both inspirational and aspirational as it shared the author's breadth of virtue which ranged from his passions in life—his family, his music, his writing, and his grit as a life-traveller.'

—Reuben Laurente
Filipino recording, performing, and visual Artist

'*Grabe itong* book *ni* Yugel on his music journey. It's like reading the screenplay of a musical. *Para akong nanood ng sine. Sobrang* vivid *ng paglalathala.* (Yugel's book on his music journey is like reading the screenplay of a musical. I feel like I'm watching a movie on the big screen. It's so vivid.)'

—Dex Facelo
Lead guitarist, vocalist, and
songwriter of pop-rock band Alamid

And for the Record

Memoir of a Filipino Writer–Musician

Yugel Losorata

PENGUIN BOOKS

An imprint of Penguin Random House

PENGUIN BOOKS

Penguin Books is an imprint of the Penguin Random House group of companies
whose addresses can be found at global.penguinrandomhouse.com

Published by Penguin Random House SEA Pte Ltd
40 Penjuru Lane, #03-12, Block 2
Singapore 609216

First published in Penguin Books by Penguin Random House SEA 2024

ISBN 9789815204933

Typeset in Garamond by MAP Systems, Bengaluru, India

www.penguin.sg

To my son, Ryde, who finds his rhythm
in basketball and family

Contents

Refrain: Syato

Chorus: Syato Reset

Bridge: The Pub Forties

Dramatis Personae

The author's list of bandmates covering the years 1996–2022, opposite their designated roles.

The Dreamers

Chris Datijan	lead vocalist, rhythm guitarist
Mike Alforte	lead guitarist
Val Crisologo	drummer
Jay Flores	lead guitarist, drummer, back-up vocals
Mike Dizon	lead guitarist
Paulo	drummer
JP Santiago	lead guitarist, vocalist
Elvin Andaya	drummer

Syato

Ronald Jayme	lead vocalist
Joseph Gonzales	guitarist, back-up vocals
Mike Santos	drummer
Jay Flores	lead guitarist
Mark Villagomez	lead vocalist
JM Delos Santos	guitarist

| Eric Villarmino | lead guitarist |
| Arly La Guardia | drummer |

Macky Brosas	drummer
Elmer Sandig	lead guitarist
Jimmy Velasquez	lead guitarist
JP Santiago	lead guitarist
Jason Pahati	guitarist

The Pub Forties

Aries Espinosa	lead vocalist
Vince Borromeo	guitarist, vocals
James Casas	drummer

Kap Aguila-Maceda	drummer
Manny Tocol	lead guitarist
Arly La Guardia	drummer

Intro

Val, our small-framed drummer boy, had the widest smile among the four of us in our college band The Dreamers back in the late 1990s. I first met him through my best friend in grade school. I had seen him a few times playing drums to accompany the choir in the Catholic church that was closest to the house where I grew up. Music helped us bond easily. My designation as the bass player put me and him together in the rhythm section, though we hardly discussed that matter as teenagers. He just rolled while I grooved, warts and all.

His laugh was contagious. It didn't matter if the joke was corny. It just felt good each time I saw his face genuinely lighten up.

But as I walked into my meeting with Val one Saturday in late 2022, two decades after The Dreamers broke up, I was shocked. The familiar smile on Val's face was no longer there. He walked slowly, like the walking dead, and I tried to make a joke out of it in a rock 'n' roll way. I felt too broken to even crack one.

I had to admit I was scared by his appearance. To say that he looked like he had gone through a lot is a total understatement. Val looked like any of these: an informal settler roaming the streets, a beggar in search of something to put into his mouth, a balding man who was about to turn into a zombie, or a person whose sanity had disappeared and who was now living in a make-believe world.

I remembered the last time I had seen him was during a reunion jam some years before. That evening he had still been pretty much himself. This time, though, even with a face mask protecting me from a world beset by Covid-19 pandemic, I couldn't get close to him.

I had heard from other people that Val had gone south after our band days, that he had marital issues. Someone said he was taking odd jobs like serving as a poll watcher or as a community night watch, colloquially termed as *barangay tanod*. They said he no longer played in the church and that he started drinking heavily. I wasn't able to confirm that myself. We never sat down to drink beer and reminisce about the past. For some reason he didn't reach out so I thought he still got it going even without music in his life.

Now, in front of me, Val held a bass guitar that looked far from being playable and needed to be tossed away, though I knew it was something of sentimental value. He had messaged me and asked if I could purchase a bass guitar in his possession, one which according to him I used to own and play with in some of our gigs long ago.

That offer from him solved a riddle that caused an old friend to hate me for years. One of my classmates from University of Santo Tomas (UST), Mabelle, let me borrow her cute-looking bass guitar for one of our college gigs. I simply forgot to return it, and Mabelle didn't confront me about it.

Years later I saw her at a concert venue when The Eraserheads (the Filipino version of The Beatles) reunited for a show called 'The Final Set'. I was excited to see her, but when I greeted her, she didn't say a word and her eyes looked away. A common friend who was with her told me later that Mabelle hated me for not handing back her bass guitar. Oh, honest mistake on my part. I thought I had returned it! My memory bank didn't help me pinpoint where I actually placed it.

That day I met Val in person for the old guitar, it suddenly dawned on me that he had had Mabelle's bass all along. I must have left it at his place after a gig or a jam session. No point in blaming Val, though, or calling Mabelle about it. She and I had already patched up during a college friend's reunion. I was forgiven without me knowing where the hell that bass guitar went.

Val, with the way he looked, had clearly suffered much in life to be even told about a bass that was supposed to be returned to its owner. It was my forgetfulness that allowed that guitar to be in his possession for years, apparently left to deteriorate in a corner of his little place, serving as a sad symbol of a dream we let go when we went our separate ways. I wasn't expecting an old instrument with rusty strings and worn-out wood turned into a piece of junk by time, or by whatever Val went through that made him look frail. I was a childhood pal looking forward to seeing a classic item that I wished to keep. Any semblance of a sweet, nostalgic meet-up vanished into thin air once I saw Val no longer looking like my old smiling friend.

I paid Val for the bass and said goodbye, walking away broken-hearted for an old mate, partly guilty over the idea that had our band somehow made it, he would have looked better that day.

I would never see Val again. He died in early 2023, and at that time I was thousands of miles away from the Philippines. I missed his funeral.

After our meet-up that had shocked me to the core, to the extent that it landed in this part of the book, I wanted to know what was going on. But I could only do so much. I was also busy preparing myself for the trip of a lifetime: to visit my mother who had relocated to the United States when I was twenty-four, around the same time The Dreamers disbanded.

The day we last saw each other, Val looked gripped by disease. It felt like he wouldn't last long, and I hate myself for being right. Bless his soul. If I could turn the clock back, I would reach out and pull him in my loop in any way.

Seeing what had happened to an ex-bandmate made me reassess life and view it from a different angle. Val had it rough. It felt like I understood more about why I still haven't found success the way I dreamed of. I'm still looking for my first big hit!

Seeing Val—ironically—made me appreciate what I have and the little things I had accomplished so far even more. Often, I find that I am too hard on myself. In a snap of a finger, I would transform from being a warrior to a worrier. That a friend I shared part of my youth with had less luck made me feel like an ungrateful jerk.

I once hoped to become a published writer and I did. My byline has been credited to hundreds or perhaps more than a thousand news articles and features, mostly about music. That's two decades plus of writing for nationally circulated newspapers and magazines, as well as online sites. The privilege enabled me to penetrate the Philippine music scene and become friends with a lot of people in and around it.

I developed into a songwriter too. It has gotten better since my college days. The five dozen songs I have a hand in writing or producing have been recorded and officially released on CDs and digital platforms. Two bands I led, Syato and The Pub Forties—which had been backed by record labels to some extent—played comparatively bigger gigs and recorded at iconic recording studios.

At times it's hard to face the fact that mainstream success is not coming my way. My wife, Kaye, said that doesn't mean I have failed. Failure doesn't exist, according to the forever young Kobe Bryant. Your little success is someone else's pinnacle of triumph. It's cliché but true that it's really not the destination but you enjoying the journey that gets you somewhere.

Being a music writer enables me to write about other people's success and get them published. Life may look easy for me, but it is the opposite. It has always been doubly hard since some people think of me as purely a music journalist, while others who knew me from way back wonder why I ventured into being an entertainment reporter when I am supposed to be the one answering questions with wit, or sheer sarcasm in the absence of wit. Acquaintances in the music industry sometimes suspect me of using my influence as a media guy to advance my motives as a musician.

Okay, that's partly true. But it's because I have to work off my strengths. I have had to go the hard way. I had to write about some stars to get to know people. I have to keep on improving as a musician to get to play my songs. Some blokes I met value my presence because I can write articles. Others think highly of what I write because I do music myself. Writing and making music are intertwined in my life, and both make me who I am.

Through it all, I believe the worth of my ride is the key starts and stops that happened along the way, which brought me to where I am now—surviving, appreciating my music, my writing, life in general, and still dreaming big.

I thank Val for the memories we shared in our youth. I want to remember him as the young, happy-go-lucky mate who would carry the same rattan backpack where he kept his battered drumsticks, and nearly nothing else. I want to cherish the happy, funny, learning times I went through with people I got to work with, bumped into, and whom I still collaborate to this day in any way possible.

You may come across some cringe moments as you read along. You'd probably wish I left some stuff on the cutting room floor. Don't worry, just take that as the bridge of a song, an interesting detour—one could say. We'll surely get back to the chorus in no time.

Some tales are bittersweet fun. Here's one that talks about bands, songs, musicians, friends, celebrities, hopes, frustrations, and life lessons. The intro's done. Time to sing.

Verse: The Dreamers

Chapter 1

Musician or Writer

I went through high school and college never seeing my name appear on a campus paper as the writer of an article. I had to go through the eye of a needle to earn my byline. In particular, it took some employees' resignation for me to get the opportunity to become a staff writer on *Manila Bulletin* for special features. It's a section not even belonging to traditional folds like sports, business, lifestyle, and entertainment. The Supplements section needed new writers and the editor, who later became a lifelong friend and mentor, thought I could write because my sales boss saw that I was better at writing proposals than actually getting clients to place advertisements for *Manila Bulletin*.

In other words, it took the gamble of a special section editor and the frustration of a marketing head for me to get my dream byline.

My first article was not about my favourite band or song. The topic was about cars, and I've never been a car person; I can't and I won't drive after a traumatizing accident while learning how to drive back in college. I was with Chris, my friend and bandmate, driving someone else's car inside a village one time after an overnight stay at our friend's house. He saw the parked car that I was about to hit. He shouted, 'Brake, brake . . .' I did exactly the opposite. I stepped on the gas!

I had to pay a few thousand pesos to the owner whose car I had smashed. My mother, she'd be pleased if I don't drive again just to ensure my safety. I have never held a steering wheel again, save for a couple of nerve-racking tries.

My wife, who is a good driver, endured my butt seated on the passenger's side for the longest time.

On the music front, observers must have thought I got too intrigued by the rock 'n' roll life with my exposure to it as a music writer, like I forced myself in by learning an instrument and trying my hand at writing lyrics.

Oh, I'm not some do-it-all guy who decided to become a rock star overnight. I've been in bands long before my destiny as a music reporter was carved. I've gone through the garage band thing, and then formed a new one after. I was leading a band of officemates by the time I wrote my first published entertainment-angled article.

Somebody asked on the lines of that proverbial which-comes-first question—chicken or egg. Am I a musician first then a writer, or vice versa?

I started writing poems when I was in high school. My pieces of verse reached the hundred mark by the time I graduated secondary school. My elder sister, Amelia, who moved to America in the mid-1990s after marrying her childhood playmate, was pivotal to my journey as a writer. As a teenager I saw her heartwarming one-page writing about her thoughts. It attracted me to the beauty of the written word.

She properly compiled my poems for safekeeping. I am not sure if those poems written by a teenager in the first half of the 1990s would ever see publication. But my effort was an indication that I had the tenacity to keep writing as a companion.

When my fascination with music began developing, my poetry writing took a backseat. I quickly found it amusing that I could actually recall the words I wrote if there was some melody accompanying it. I practically dropped poetry for songwriting.

As it turned out, I became a professional writer first before I started getting paid as a musician.

My two older brothers had something to do with my passion for music. Back in fourth grade, Boyet, the oldest, asked me to watch a documentary about The Beatles. I fell asleep to the clip of the Fab Four performing 'And I Love Her'. I woke up with the said tune in my head and it was my first significant LSS (Last Song Syndrome) experience.

With The Beatles at the centre of my awakening as a music enthusiast, my childhood was filled with music from cassette tapes and 45s of groups like Air Supply, Queen, and ABBA played in repeat mode. Those songs would put me in a trance.

I wrote my first song in 1992, perhaps a year after I started penning poems. The tune to that song I called 'You're My Soul' remained in my mind, though I haven't bothered to put chords to it until today. In the beginning I would only compose melodies without knowing how to play it. It was only in college when I started adding chords to the songs I made.

There was nothing extraordinary about how I first mated with writing and music. But my entry into the world of music press and my eventual growth in my journey to become a recording artist cleared my path. It really did not matter which of the two was more important. I wanted to be a writer-musician or a musician-writer.

There is always fun experiencing life when you are traversing two rivers. Few people would say they're both onstage and backstage. Performers see their dressing room as the place of calm before the storm. I see it as a spot to discover interesting lives and thoughts from celebrities I get to interview. On the other hand, personal attendants may view the stage as an unconquerable frontier. I felt that thing emitted through the smokescreen right on my face. I dealt with blinking lights as I kept my fingers pressed to root notes ensuring the proper bass lines.

I can think of celebrated Filipinos who have lived life like me: Lourd De Veyra, Francis Reyes, and Joey Dizon, to name a few. These guys can rock the world and bring the news. But unlike me, they're kind of household names—rock stars and respected by industry insiders. I find myself in the middle earth of where they are. I am not a rock star, not a celebrated journalist. I am just your regular guy who happened to have enjoyed a little bit of the limelight.

Chapter 2

Heartbeat

When someone asks what major I took in college, I always wish I could say I had gone to a music conservatory. In truth, I chose Political Science. My father wanted me to become a lawyer.

In the Philippines, to graduate from college is a life prerequisite, and people look down on dropouts. Once I got a diploma, I didn't take it further. I wanted to pursue the arts, specifically, the writer's life. I was born a middle child, the fifth of nine siblings. I grew up the quiet one who hardly spoke, but deep inside I wanted to express my feelings and thoughts. Thus, my strong need to write them. Initially, I stuck with what my father wanted.

I lost the drive to become a lawyer by the time I graduated from the University of Santo Tomas. No thanks to spending two years in Pol. Sci. class watching my classmates debate about the constitutionality of electing a class president while the term of a previously elected one wasn't over. Or being invited to join an activist's group worrying about tuition hike or the government succumbing to the alleged bullying of a superpower nation. I found it hypocritical to act scholarly or pretend to know the social issues of the time when my ultimate concern was how to make my crush fall for me or get to record a song I wrote. At the time, I was hell-bent on pursuing music to become a recording artist. I never expected to be doing the singer-songwriter beat. I wanted to be part of a band with an album—touring and gigging.

While in campus, I was aiming to get into literary circles and establish a name either as a poet or a short story writer. It didn't help that a year after I graduated from university, I still hadn't landed a job. My mother tried to endorse me to her friend for a slot at NFA (National Food Authority). I went through the process of applying, only to be turned down in the end. I remember the day I knew all my efforts were for naught. I was so frustrated and disoriented that I asked the elevator person if she could take me to the ground floor. Somebody laughed because it was common sense, it's going down there. I wanted to laugh at myself, too, but I was very mad. It's a mad world.

I started working at a fast-food outlet in Tandang Sora, Quezon City. As I was mopping the floor, I saw a high school batchmate enter the store and line up to order food. I shivered, fearing that I'd be seen and become the subject of ridicule among our circle. I imagined them laughing—the boy from the star section now cleaning up a diner! I hid in the back area and waited until my batchmate left. I didn't go back the following day, feeling the risk of being seen by someone I know.

Not long after that day, I received a call from *Manila Bulletin*—the result of a folded resume I dropped at its booth at a job fair at Megamall in Ortigas. My first thought was: working for the nation's leading newspaper ensured that I was at the doorstep of a journalist's career. But the Human Resources representative could only offer an entry-level post in the marketing department. I had to be a journalism graduate to qualify as a reporter (Read: I didn't choose journalism partly because I was avoiding a girl I was infatuated with, who had rejected me. See, this girl from college broke my heart not once, but twice!).

The marketing boss of a special feature department, Badette Cunanan, took me in to be part of her staff of account executives. Ooh, sounds corporate. But that meant I'd be working as a marketing person, convincing clients to place ads in the broadsheet.

The *Bulletin* opening was a very big news for me. I was so positive about it that I was already imagining myself having a byline, forgetting for a second that I wasn't even hired as a writer. It would take time to see my name below the title of an article. I was determined to prove I could write for a newspaper.

Looking back, I now wondered if the best option would have been to go to law school. My parents were willing to finance my schooling had I expressed interest. But I wanted to write and make music, period. From the time I stepped in *Manila Bulletin* for my first day at work in March 2000, everything in my life tended to revolve around my passion for writing and music. You bet it's risky to have endeavours that don't pay well, especially since I'm Filipino and the Philippines is a country where young poets are described as hungry. There even was a band called Hungry Young Poets led by Barbie Almalbis, who went on to rank amongst the top rock queens of the country. And as you can guess, paid gigs are minimal, especially for unknown bands like the one I was in at the time, The Dreamers. Good pay was only for acts with hit songs or acts that could deliver three sets of covers while also juggling customer requests.

But you see, I didn't have a choice either. I was born to write words and make melodies.

Yugel Losorata in one of his early gigs with The Dreamers (circa late 1990s)

Chapter 3

Second Fiddle

Why join a band if you can make music by yourself in the comfort of your living room? Your bedroom, if you want to make it more private. Then if you want to, you can board a cab with your guitar and go to a joint and sing a composition you can say was written by you just hours ago. And you can debut it in front of your drunken friends, who are likely to be willing to clap their hands for you, especially if you are shouldering their drinks.

Well, joining a band can be more fun. Can't argue with that. When you're crafting a song with your bandmates and you're seeing it take shape in a full-on recording, the feeling is tantric and you can rest assured that if you hear it a decade after, you would relive the bliss of how it was created, how it came to be through the synergy of some young talents.

The Beatles felt for Elvis Presley not because their fame had already overshadowed him when they met in August 1965, but because he experienced the mayhem without having anyone to share it with. It was only him and his Memphis Mafia of yes men. The moptops went through it, either lying on top of each other to beat the cold air on their journey to the Decca Records audition, or locking themselves in the same room as a four-headed monster. There is unity in diversity.

In the line-up of the four bands that I have joined—or may I say, formed myself, with the help of a co-equal—I acted as the band leader to a great extent, even though all four had a legitimate front man.

The kind and clean-cut Chris Datijan, whom I first met on 6 October 1995, was acknowledged by our peers to be the main man in our college group The Dreamers. He had the look and character, with his pale skin and moody stare. His glasses alone made him Lennonesque. It was a good thing he didn't push himself to act in a very Lennon way. He was no rebel, and was, in fact, very romantically expressive. He never failed to shower his object of affection with flowers, and he had a number of songs titled after girls: 'Abigail', 'Audrey', and 'Michelle' are just a few examples of what we had in our repertoire. We tried presenting ourselves as a little parody of Lennon and McCartney. It was partly for that reason that I had to take the bass guitar as my instrument. I had to be Paul.

Back in the heady days of the '90s it was cool to be a rock fan and mimic the voice and ways of Axl Rose or Kurt Cobain. The latter had already passed when we formed our college band. Chris and I—and others like us—went against the tide, we went backwards. We loved the '60s largely because of The Beatles. We both wanted to be in a band because of our obsession with the music and ideals of The Fab Four. It was certainly not a bad choice of influence on how I wished to lead my life. I was thrilled to be in a band, not because of the booze or chicks, but because I simply fell for the wonder of creating music with the hope of getting the adulation of audiences.

Chris and I were both freshmen at UST when we met. He was playing guitar under a tree after our Physical Education (PE) class and singing 'I Want to Hold Your Hand' with Jay Flores, another eventual band member. I was hooked. This was the song that had welcomed The Beatles in America, and into the consciousness of the world. I introduced myself and declared that I was a Beatles fan. Someone later tried to be cute, cutting me out by mockingly butting in, 'Who isn't.' But Chris knew what I meant by that. I wasn't a regular fan trying to get attention. I wanted to write songs with him.

The three of us—Chris, Jay, and I—would become bandmates under a name that I had suggested. A classmate of mine in Pol. Sci. class asked about our purpose of forming a band. I answered, '*Wala eh*, we're dreamers' (nothing much, we're dreamers). Chris and Jay seemed to like that, and we decided to call ourselves The Dreamers. To this day I can't forgive us for not coming up with a better name.

It's easy to form a band. You only need to find an equal and push forth the idea that you're co-leaders. Arguably it's unlikely that a band would have two blokes calling the shots, for often there's the main man and then his roborats. But the two-headed monster for a leader set-up works for me. There's less pressure if you share leadership. More importantly, I get a boost when I play the strong second fiddle—the second billing guy who in some occasions outmanoeuvres the person deemed as the front man.

Chapter 4

Soundtrack of Our Youth

Chris and I were, in the truest sense, best of friends. We were both Beatlemaniacs and liked to develop our songwriting.

It was a no-brainer that we decided on crediting every song we wrote to Chris-Yugel. It was a songwriting partnership only we two cared about, to put it bluntly. At that time in our late teens, it kept our friendship solid.

We wrote songs everywhere—in his room in their apartment in M. Hizon St in Manila, at our sala in La Trinidad Village in Quezon City, right outside of the rehearsal studio where we were scheduled to practise songs, and even in certain spots at UST. One song called 'Lumipas Na Eksena' mentioned Tinoco Park, a spot frequented by activists. Chris started with the verses and I felt compelled to contribute significantly. I came up with a chorus and the song became a legitimate 50/50 collaboration. Like Lennon and McCartney, the reason I came to love collaborative songwriting was my work with him, many of our songs were written largely by one of us, with contributions from the other one.

For the first four songs by The Dreamers, Chris wrote most of 'Ordinary Day' and 'Mine', which I described as very Chris, while I penned something called 'Saved by the Bell'. 'Ask Me Again', which Chris supplemented with a refrain part, became our first real collaboration as songwriters. It was actually the first song I wrote that I offered to the group rounded up by Jay on drums. The Dreamers began as a trio and we really didn't have a lead guitarist so Jay would also play lead guitar in the demos.

I thought Chris was ahead of me even in the songwriting department. It took a while for me to get my bearings and only when I penned 'Something Big' and started writing 'Nawawalang Sulat' did I feel my confidence coming in. 'Something Big' was described by one of our friends as a B-side piece, but Chris and I loved singing it, with its charging tempo and happy vibe. 'When you're feeling down / Don't hesitate just call out my name . . .' goes the chorus. It felt fine being able to inject my love for books in the latter part of the chorus. 'Thank you, my baby, 'cause you're all I need / Like a pretty book I'm beggin' to read all the time.'

Hearing Chris coming in to harmonize in the chorus was priceless.

'Nawawalang Sulat' was inspired songwriting for someone just starting out. I was cleaning out a room in our house one time when I found a letter from a high school classmate. It was a letter penned as homework. One of our teachers grouped us as partners and asked that we write letters to each other. My partner was the class secretary, so I benefited from her good penmanship. The letter looked nice, and its content sounded sincere. It was enough for me to come up with the idea of a guy reading a letter he thought he'd lost and realizing, after reading it, that his girlfriend had already left him for another boy.

Chris supplied the song with a sort of bridge that detoured from the verses and refrain that pushed the narrative and made the track melancholic. It was a song with Tagalog/Filipino lyrics, and it paved the way for our band to go past old school rock 'n' roll and venture into alternative rock. Our other Tagalog compositions like 'JS' and 'Plastik', both songs I largely wrote on the same day after coming home from school and riffing alone in our place in Barangay Talipapa, got us further deep into the kind of rock prevalent in the '90s Philippine band scene.

My songwriting partner had a special interest in 'JS'; he came up with a guitar riff that was simply amazing and introduced the song on a high note.

Chris and I would call each other using landlines to share notes. I can't forget how excited his voice was every time he rang to share a melody or lyric or line he just came up with. While always on the same page, I could see the differences in our style. He more or less kept the '60s feel in songs he mainly penned, like in 'Bahay Blues' and 'Galaw', both of which we played a lot of times in our gigs. I veered away from very Chris songs. That was evident with one called 'Telebabad', where my funky bass line Chris complemented with wah-wah infused rhythm guitar playing. 'Domeng' (a slang for dirty old man) was another song that was influenced more by Eraserheads instead of any '60s act.

It's a pity that none of these songs I mentioned were ever recorded formally. There were two Chris-Yugel songs that Syato, my second band, later released, but I'd rather not compare The Dreamers rough versions of 'Elkyu' and 'Panaginip Lamang'.

I still hope that one day, some young band or solo artist will get hold of some Chris-Yugel songs and record them. It would be interesting how songs written by two friends who were young and promising in the '90s would be interpreted by ultra-modern kids.

On the other hand, I'm not losing hope that one day Chris and I would find ourselves in the same country or city and pull in Mike and Jay to record what Chris labelled as the 'Soundtrack of Our Youth'.

Chapter 5

Funky Calls

There's really something very cool about being in a band than doing it solo. The best times of The Dreamers were spent during days when we would jam after school, playing while still in uniform. In the final two years of our days together, we were also facing the real world, especially for me and Chris, the band's one-two punch, schoolmates and batchmates, it was a pretty odd time to have to look for a break in the band scene while also trying to locate our path after graduation.

Chris and I wrote the songs, and naturally, in such a set-up, the composer sings his songs as he knows them more than anyone else, although in truth you really can't guess who's going to best interpret a particular song. It may be an artist you like the least.

Being young and immature, I got infuriated when both Michael and Val suggested that Chris should be the sole singer. I should just focus on the bass, an instrument rarely associated with a band leader. That was another way of saying I couldn't sing. I knew in my heart that I could. I was not just technically gifted. It would take years before singing would become a weapon in my arsenal of musicianship. Years later a record producer would give me a little pat on the shoulder by saying that I am a living example of how one improves his game by experience.

As for me wanting to sing co-lead as part of The Dreamers, well, you can't blame me. One, I was still too young to realize I wasn't lead vocalist material. Two, Chris and I were trying to be like Lennon and McCartney. That couldn't happen if I'd solely play the bass.

The years of trying to create my spot as a singing bass player proved useful. I transformed into a back-up singer. That gave my compositions the quality of being vocal-driven. More often than not, there would be harmonies in the recorded tracks of my later bands.

Early on I developed the attitude of letting my bass lines walk, perhaps to compensate for my lack of vocal strength. Obviously, Sir Paul McCartney has always been a major musical influence to me and the Knight's bass playing really sings. If you listen to records where I play bass, you'd probably notice that I tend to move my fingers on the frets for action. As much as possible, I see to it that my bass lines do not get in the way of the other instruments. I believe that a bass part should do its job by speaking on its own without being bothersome to others. Cannot talk at the same time.

There are also instances when the bass player just needs to keep himself grounded on root notes. If you have nothing good to offer to make your lines busy, stay where you should be and keep the song in the proper groove.

I wrote 'Telebabad' and it showcased the funkiest bass line I could ever come up with. Chris liked it enough and it received constant praise from him. I can't recall if I did ask him to sing it but on the demo we did, he sang the track while I happily delivered on the four strings.

The song was inspired by my teenage routine of having phone pals. Back in the '90s we did that to hook up with the opposite sex. Befriend someone over the phone, via landline as there were no cell phones yet, before meeting up with them. There was this girl I enjoyed talking to and she projected herself as a typical nice girl. We dated and I thought we could really end up as lovers. We seemed to like each other even after seeing each other's faces.

One night I traced that she was working at a pub house as a G.R.O. That stands for Guest Relations Officer, which sounds decent if not for the fact it became an acronym for a girl who entertains customers that buy her ridiculously pricey drinks in the hope of getting her to some motel after. I wasn't fine with having a G.R.O for a girlfriend. That was a conviction I had back then, considering a G.R.O is likely to be the muse of some drunken customer who wants to get laid. We may be talking about a variety of bar patrons.

I do believe that in liking a girl, her past or her work shouldn't matter. But, well, I was quite conservative in those days and I would have rather had someone who was not working in the skin trade.

Still, I am a hopeless romantic, and I believe that in loving someone you love all of them, whatever they are.

What I didn't like was being lied to. What else could she be hiding?

My 'Telebabad' experience was a string of nights talking to strangers in sexy bedroom voices. One time I thought a phone pal would look pretty, only to feel disappointed when I eventually met her. My perception of beauty as a youngster was quite racist, as most people in the Philippines who are unaware of this are. We see pale-skinned and sharp-nosed people as more beautiful than those who are not.

Once I found myself in the presence of a beautiful, tall girl with long, straight hair. It was a stroke of bad luck when I realized I didn't have any money to even buy her a burger! I was a college boy with usually just enough for transportation fare to reach school and get back home after. I then decided that I needed to be prepared for moments like this and ask my parents—ahead of time—to give me extra cash. A friend brought her to school to meet me without informing me beforehand. I wanted to cry seeing her, she was so beautiful and I didn't have a penny for a date!

Certainly, my chorus lines '*Kinikilig tuwing kausap*' (Feeling flattered while we're talking) and '*Di makatulog naririnig ka*' (Can't sleep for I'm hearing you) for 'Telebabad' fitted this girl named Juliet. In those days we didn't have the luxury of checking someone's looks with a mere click. I had no access to Juliet's photograph so I didn't really realize that the voice on the other line was a beauty in person.

The Dreamers could have jammed to 'Telebabad' well, but we ran out of time. We only started jamming to the song as we were about to call it quits. It came too late in our run. I wonder about how it would sound if we had pushed through and focused on polishing the song. Often, a song I associate with a past band gets stuck to it and I don't bother introducing it to the new band. So, the members of Syato, my second band, never got to hear it and the song remained unrecorded. It's one of those tracks Chris and I would pluck if and when we would sit down together and commit ourselves to finally putting our compositions on tape.

'Telebabad' is basically mine, but with Chris' deep care for it and key suggestions to improve the song, it's a beautiful piece of collaboration as far as I know. That's the beauty of having a songwriting partner for a bandmate. It's always more fun if there are two of you who are really excited about a new creation and won't mind owning the song as a partnership. That's another logical reason as to why I usually don't touch the twenty-five songs I wrote during my time with Chris. It's my way of respecting the partnership even if our group didn't make it in the fame game. Having Chris on board was special for me, and it's sad that our partnership, to be frank about it, ended up as a footnote in my life.

Chapter 6

Whistleblower

My father, Eulogio Sr., or 'Papa', as we his many children address him—not 'daddy' as we thought that's for super rich fathers, nor *tatay* since we do feel we're not that impoverished—had an interesting way of calling us when he needed us for whatever reason, whether it be some assistance with his own house's carpentry, or to give him a massage on his forehead. He would whistle our names instead of calling them.

Each kid had a designated whistle tune that Papa came up with himself. My seafaring old man was composing melodies! That was my earliest exposure to songwriting, I guess. The whistle he assigned to me was a bit more melodious than the others because it had a really good recall. For me, it seemed more inventive than the ones for my siblings. Accuse me of being biased. But that happened by chance. There was no favouritism surrounding those whistle tunes.

Sadly, I wasn't able to put on record his voice whistling. What a miss that I didn't pursue the idea when he and Mama came back to Manila for a visit, twice. It would have been fun if I was able to ask him to record that sound coming from his mouth. I'm not sure if Papa saw my passion for music early on, but I won't forget the moment he bought me a keyboard. In some instances, he would strike a conversation about music, like he'd express his amusement over the falsettos of the Bee Gees, or the fine harmonies of The Beatles.

One day, out of the blue, while I was seated in the *sala* and he was done watching the news, Papa shared, 'I was a teenager in Palompon, Leyte. We would go to a party and during the sweet dance they played "Girl." Those harmonies by The Beatles made those moments extra exciting.'

He knew I was developing an interest in The Beatles and for music in general.

I wished I'd asked him what his influence was for his whistles. To this day I know his whistle for me by heart, and I intend to have it as an intro to a recording soon.

My father, with my mother, Amalia—Amy for short—had lived in the United States for the last nineteen years of his life.

Ryde, my kid, did get into one of my recordings after I pulled him in during a session when he was about four years old. I asked him to say something on the microphone as the recording button was on inside the Amerasian Studio in Scout Madrinan, Quezon City. I was with my then band Syato, recording a track I co-wrote with rapper friend Blanktape, called 'Tulay'.

Ryde uttered his favourite expression at the time, 'What you say?', towards the end of the song, or before the banter between our lead singer—my brother-in-law Mark Villagomez—and Blanktape to close out the song.

One guy steps on a male ego by becoming the lover of the girl his friend fantasizes about. It happened to me for real back in college. I asked a classmate-buddy to endorse me to a girl I liked. I thought his closeness to her would help my cause. Apparently, they were too close. They ended up having a child!

If Ryde could whistle, I would have asked him to do so on record. I want to have a track where someone's whistling is prominent, like in the band True Faith's 'Huwag Na Lang Kaya' or Rivermaya's 'Bring Me Down'. John Lennon whistled rightfully in the fade out for 'Two of Us'. It enhanced the feeling of 'riding nowhere' conveyed in the song.

I'm amused by my father's ability to whistle. He made use of it in a musical sense. It's his lone strength in the music department but it strongly showed me the value of recall. If those whistles had no recall, there would have been some whipping that went on in the household because one of my brothers would fail to respond to his call. I don't know any daddy who whistles to call his children. For that, Papa's kind of unique. And despite my musical inclination, it's funny that I can't whistle myself.

Papa was never expressive of his take on my musicianship. He wanted me to become a lawyer and even offered to finance my law schooling. I begged off because I knew in my heart it was not my calling and I was afraid to flunk the bar exam. I do have some regret not trying it after majoring in Pol. Sci., which is a natural prerequisite for students aiming to be lawyers. Earning money would have been easier if I took up law and he surely would have been happy to see me earn a title.

But going through that path may have pulled me away from making music.

Again, Papa's one gesture showed that he took my decision well. He bought me a keyboard.

Playing a Hofner bass at Minokaua bar in the City of Manila

Chapter 7

Songs from My Childhood

Songwriting can be improved through self-learning or by attending workshops. But first you gotta have it in you. It should come naturally out of your head. You were born to do it.

Your inclination towards certain types of music determines the kind of songs you will write. As a child, I had been exposed to classic pop or rock. There are four acts whose music I was consistently hearing as a youngster without being conscious about it: The Beatles, Queen, ABBA, and Air Supply.

The *Greatest Hits I* from Queen boasted a very strong line-up; the two follow-up collections are nowhere near half as good despite having classics on their own. My two older brothers *kuya* Boyet and kuya Boygic must have been playing the tape on repeat on an old cassette or on the vinyl as I—a young boy with no awareness of the music scene—somehow knew that 'Bohemian Rhapsody' is followed by 'Another One Bites the Dust'. One afternoon they asked me to sit down as they were sound-trippin.

'Pakinggan mo to' (Listen to this), they both urged.

Then they did something on the record that altered the voice of Freddie Mercury, Queen's vocalist. Instead of hearing him sing the title of the hit song, I heard the flamboyant front man utter, 'It's fun to smoke marijuana.' The sound was weird and was not too clear. It was a bit scary, and it somehow ruined my perception of the track as a danceable tune.

Later as a grown up, I was convinced that these supposed diabolical lines were nothing but coincidence. It's like seeing a face on the moon or a scary figure out of billowing fire smoke.

ABBA songs, on the other hand, were my first exposure to real pop songs. For the longest time I thought 'Chiquitita' was their signature piece, not 'Dancing Queen', as I later learned. 'Money, Money, Money' really made a big impression on me, particularly the voice on the verses, which I thought sounded sexy and were pushed on by the thumping accompaniment. It created a sense of foreboding, which made the song more interesting.

And then there's Air Supply, whose love songs became my initial understanding of music as a medium for sentimentality. Back then I could hardly differentiate their songs. I couldn't tell 'Come What May' from 'Here I Am' until much later when I began checking out titles and lyrics. The duo had a string of hits. Often, I would hear this set on repeat, the repetition not ever bothering me. When I was in high school, there was one more gem they came out with, fittingly titled 'Goodbye'. The piano riff grabbed my attention immediately.

Both Queen and ABBA had scored their last major hits in the '80s. 'Goodbye' was a new single from Air Supply in the early '90s and it was as good as any of their previous hits. I was witnessing the birth of a classic! That was the same feeling when Fra Lippo Lippi's 'Stitches and Burns' came out. It was an instant gem for the old soul—even if it was new then.

The Beatles had come to me, they had been a part of my life even before I knew it. I had been humming the intro line to 'Girl' for as long as I can remember. Initially I got it wrong, like 'Is there anybody who wants to set me free' instead of 'Is there anybody going to listen to my story'. I misheard the lyric; the first of many times. When I began my deep dive into the band, devouring anything written about them, I remember one piece saying that such an opening line was the most ironic ever in the history of pop because everybody wanted to listen to the man who wrote the song and he was asking if there's anyone who would care to.

My wife, Kaye, my version of the 'girl who came to stay', described Lennon's line as the most arresting she had ever heard—thanks to the split-second late entry of the instrumental accompaniment. It gave John Lennon's voice the spotlight in all its vulnerable splendour.

The Beatles were the biggest of them all and no one should argue about that. One time it was a piece of controversial news when somebody said that One Direction would be bigger. My reaction was the same as that of the announcer after witnessing Damien Lillard hit a trey from midcourt over the stretch arms of Paul George: Are you kidding me?

Chris once wondered why I was so into the '80s. He found the age of synthesizers fake and preferred the cerebral force of electric or acoustic guitar.

We didn't argue about it. I embraced the '80s for its beautiful, high recall melodies. There's something in the way Duran Duran cooks up the ingredients in their arrangements. Their melodies found home in my head, taking me back to younger years—with my soundtripping older brothers.

Nothing beats childhood memories regardless of how wealthy or poor your family is at such a critical period in your life. They're like sweet dreams you want to replay over and over in your sleep. The music that reminds you of such times will always be important to you.

One time when we were in the big house of our aunt in Marikina (the city where I was born), I found myself in the company of '80s teenagers, the Bagets generation as they were called—Bagets was a quintessential film.

The front yard had been turned into a disco house complete with strobe lights and a mobile playing the era's current hits. I witnessed teens partying to the tune of Industry's 'State of the Nation'. That band was a one-hit wonder and their song was definitive '80s. The cliché line 'There's no place like home' fitted the song. That night really felt like home thanks to the music and vibe.

Chapter 8

My Past Sounds Familiar

Some songs—current radio hits or blasts from the past—get stuck to something or someone I've seen or known. It's automatic; it's impossible to undo the connection. The power of certain pieces of music to connect is proof that melodies and memories come together and don't let go.

One girl from high school, Aileen Loreto, comes to mind when I hear the danceable early '90s hit 'Finally' by Cece Peniston. I heard the track one time while looking at her, or I must have first encountered the song on the radio while thinking about her. We were in first year of high school and I thought we were connected, possible soulmates. But then I found out she was linked to a boy named Phyll whom I actually looked up to because he could play the guitar very well and was among the boys considered cool in our school.

With zero confidence, I found it best to stay away than be pitted against Phyll. Years later I would jam with him and a couple of other high school classmates at his work place; he had become a government office executive. I still felt privileged that I was jamming with Phyll. If you were a nerd back in school, the inferiority complex naturally comes back in the presence of someone like him.

In college, my head turned to a hot-looking girl right on the first day of school. It was obvious she would become the muse of our class, with her long hair, curvy figure, and overall classic beauty, a kind that didn't fizzle out even semesters after. She was a member of UST's premier dance troupe, and I had to forever attach her to another dance track—the bass line-powered 'Short Short Man', or that sexy tune with stupid lyrics that talked about small dicks.

If I hear the song on some retro radio station, I could still see her moving her hips to the groove of the bass. It would have been more appropriate if I instead associated her with a sweet love song. It wasn't meant to be. She had to be the girl behind the short, short man!

Anyway, let's move on to love songs. Weddings are events best for slow, heartfelt songs. I'm reminded of the wedding of my brother kuya Boygic and his wife, Sheryl, when I hear of 'Lady' by Kenny Rogers. Sometime after their wedding reception, I heard 'Lady' being played and I thought it fitted well to the occasion.

The wedding ceremony for my sister Beverly and her husband, Ted, had been frozen in my head to the tune of 'Looking Through the Eyes of Love' by Melissa Manchester. Again, sometime during the celebration, the song was played.

One song in high school made me recall the whole period partly because the number never became as classic as the other '90s hits. It went off with the times. That's why during a family gathering, when I sang on a karaoke the old hit 'Deep in My Soul' by Acosta-Russell, one of the teenage girls approached me and said that it was a good song. It was the first time she had heard the piece that used to be the song in my head when I was thinking of Victoria Gabriel, my ultimate high school crush. She was my crush until I learned she'd become pregnant.

The track happened to be a big hit when I was in second year high school, a period when my infatuation for Victoria was at its peak.

Being in high school in the '90s turned some songs into mementos of people I used to be friends with. Edward Romero was a boy hard to forget as he was a rare, straitlaced lad. One time I saw him crying inside our classroom after everyone else had left the room. I must have forgotten something, so I had gone back to look for it. I approached him and asked what was wrong. He said it's because of his love for a batchmate named Julie Ann Pet. His tears were real. A few days later, he asked me if I'd heard a song by the Williams Brothers called 'Can't Cry Hard Enough'. I had not.

After hearing him sing the song with a guitar, I felt so moved I told him that we should form a duo. We did sort of become bandmates when two others expressed wanting to form a band with us.

That same school year, there was the big Introvoys hit, 'Will I Survive', which reached top two in DJ Triggerman's WLS FM's OPM year-end countdown for 1992. The number one is another song from the same band, called 'Di Na Ko Aasa Pa'.

I'd forever call 'Will I Survive' the Jacqueline Peralta song, the acknowledged dream girl of our batch. Thanks to how impassioned Ford, a boy who had a deep crush on her, was expressing his infatuation for her. He told me he was dedicating the song to her. 'I can't get you out of my mind', says one line in the song. One time, I chatted with Ford, and he was praising Jacqueline to no end. His face was glowing just mentioning her name.

One morning during a flag ceremony in school, somebody pushed the wrong button. Instead of playing the national anthem, it played the song. We all heard the intro and the oohs and aahs were classic. We were teenagers highly romanticizing love songs. That boy could have collapsed at that moment. Pure adolescent bliss.

The love struck teenager's affection for Jacqueline was not reciprocated. Ouch. But I was happy to know years later that Ryan went on to have a happy, quiet life in Canada. He survived.

College days: Yugel Losorata (above left) with The Dreamers bandmates (clockwise) Mike Alforte, Chris Datijan, and Val Crisologo

Chapter 9

Demo Days

Back in college, doing a song demo meant making original music in its raw state, a quality that can't pass proper recording standards. We demoed once at the jamming place we frequented back in the mid-to-late '90s, called Red Damien in Barangay Bahay Toro in Quezon City. I had so many memories there. Even some of the early Syato rehearsals were spent in that small room of band instruments, including that evening when record producer Snaffu Rigor christened us as Syato.

Red Damien is basically a studio inside the owner's garage. It's a room where us Dreamers practised, often just the four of us.

We demoed a song called 'Classmate', which I largely wrote. The funny thing was, while it was meant to be a duet song between me and Chris, the finished demo only had us properly harmonizing on the last line. It was crap!

But in hindsight, since there was no autotune at that time, it meant we really hit it well on that final line. Years later, with Syato, I'd savour the times I'd hear us voicing right on the dot. We sounded good and I was the third wheel in the blending of voices.

The Dreamers were in essence a demo band. We never came to a point of recording a song we thought was of quality good enough to be played on FM radio. Those five or six years we were together could be boiled down to one cheap cassette demo of twelve songs, special to us if I may say. Good compositions, but poorly recorded. It's not in the playing or singing, but in how they were mixed. Back then, when a band said it's going to make a demo, you'd hear a sub-standard quality, unlike in the twenty-first century when a studio could produce a demo passable for official release or radio airplay.

An early version of 'Elkyu' was demoed at Ted Reyes' house. Ted was the heart and soul of The Free Souls whose members were our big brothers, who influenced our way of doing music and dressing up. They wore turtlenecks.

At a home studio in Manila owned by one Nolit Abanilla who would turn out to be a lifelong friend and a key figure in the independent music scene in the Philippines, we put on tape a demo composed of our earliest compositions. Jay played drums and lead guitar. In between takes he'd share rock 'n' roll stories he had read. His expression, 'Talo', which he said to mean something is a downer, became our group's favourite reaction to all things that we felt didn't appear or sound right.

There were magical moments when an accident or mistake made a song special. Our demo of 'Lumipas Na Eksena' had serendipitously captured the barking of a dog before Chris began singing the line '*Ayoko nang makinig sayo*'. To me, it was poignant to have that bark in. Stray dogs are common in the Philippines, called *askals*. The bark came in just in time when Nolit pushed the recording button on, and before Chris began singing. It felt like our band was out in the streets and wrapping up the night after a good chat and drink.

I like hearing that demo because it's one of our best songs, a fifty-fifty collaboration. I came up with just the right chorus to Chris' already emphatic stanzas. His verses had a lot of drama in them; it was quite a challenge to have it paired with an equally strong chorus. I feel happy that I delivered with a chorus even more singable than the beautiful verses. For me, it was simply the best Chris-Yugel song. How pitiful that we could only demo it.

Chapter 10

Debut Party Band

Back in college, there was one band performance I participated in that didn't include Chris Datijan. That one was specifically set for the debut party of one of my classmates in the freshmen class of 1A2. That was the most memorable class I had been a part of.

After high school, where I was perceived as one among the nerds and endured a socially challenging life, I tried getting along with some cool characters in the university. I really didn't feel I belonged until freshman year in college.

It meant so much belonging to the group that played a few cover songs at a hotel party for Emilie Noche. Two years prior, I missed out on being onstage with some boys performing in front of our high school batchmates in St James (a private school along Tandang Sora). I had zero chance of becoming part of the bunch anyway. I couldn't play the bass at that time. In high school there were a handful of competent guitar players and it was unlikely that you'd get the slot. I knew from the start I could never be a drummer (hand and feet coordination problem, I guess) and neither was the keyboard the instrument a high schooler would wish to play in a guitar group.

Before Emilie's big night, there was a series of rehearsals that often extended to some beer joints. Our circle of friends were a mix of boys and girls who found common ground. The members of our band were me on bass, leader-of-the-pack Tony Padrinao on drums, our resident clown Mark De Leon on guitar, and two girls from our group who were the lead singers.

Another boy was also playing rhythm guitar during practices, but for some reason he didn't join the performance. I thought it benefited us that there was only one guitarist because we sounded better. I could hear the separation of instruments much clearer instead of two guitars overlapping. Years later, in a professional set-up, having two guitarists in the band could still be a problem at times unless the lead guitarist was keen enough to just play when it was time to.

Tony had to suggest a band name just for that gig: Sweet Attitudes. It became a private joke as it sounded like a show band's name. Show bands in the Philippines are known for covering songs mainly, without ever recording a composition of their own.

Sweet Attitudes performed 'Don't Speak' by No Doubt, which was a major hit at that time. Both Mark and Tony were into feel-good hits from the '80s, like Kalapana's 'Hurt' and Rex Smith's 'Simply Jessie'. We played both songs.

Chris, who was from another section, may have found our preferences odd. Him and I would bore Sweet Attitudes with our originals.

On our way out of the hotel, while inside the elevator, one of the guests recognized us. That person praised our playing. He said he liked classics. If he only knew that I would have wanted to play Beatles songs! I was in no way the leader in Sweet Attitudes. I was just happy to be part of the gang, playing bass.

The rehearsals allowed us to get closer as friends. We would laugh at how Marc—the other guitarist who didn't perform on the big night—played the D chord in a peculiar way. I couldn't copy it myself. Marc was like me, low-profile and soft-spoken. He was a pretty boy and unsurprisingly he became the boyfriend of another classmate named Beverly Flores. She was a crush of mine. I even wrote a corny poem inspired by her and titled it 'Beverly Flowers'.

I was happy to be part of the hipsters.

Back in the first day in UST, I befriended Marvin Matias who later became our batch's magna cum laude. I often dropped by his boarding house for extended chats. When he delivered a speech on graduation day, it felt nice. I was one of his first friends in college. We were seatmates, and to my luck he was a big fan of the Beatles too.

Naturally I drifted away from Marvin because I was busy being with friends who used to drink and play music. He was too studious for the kind of people I wanted to belong to.

I made sure to be friends with Christine Lising, the female alpha of the class, and Tony, her counterpart.

Years later I pulled in Tony in Syato when we were looking for a drummer. He was too into showband to go with our routine of doing originals. If only he gave more focus Tony may have ended up as a folk singer in a bar. I myself didn't like the idea of Tony being a sidekick in my band. The ringleader can't just be the drummer!

During my Dreamers days I invited Mark and Tony to play with me and Chris in a Battle of the Bands competition. We lost the competition and I thought we played out of tune. My parents were there to see us perform, and I wouldn't forget what my mother said after our spot. '*Kayo pa din ang pinakamagaling*.' (You're still the best.)

The competition's winner was a band that played a rock rendition of a Filipino hit called 'Sino Ang Baliw' (Who's crazy?) written by songwriter Mon Del Rosario who some years later served as a judge for a televised songwriting festival in which I joined and won at least in the weekly challenge.

The group that covered 'Sino Ang Baliw' performed impressively, and my admiration for my mother deepened.

The Dreamers at their usual rehearsal place Red Damien Studio in Quezon City, Philippines

Chapter 11

Disharmony

When you're in a band, there's bound to be tension among bandmates. It makes the experience more thrilling and unpredictable, as opposed to being solo when, while you do have total control, you don't have someone telling you you're going overboard. That was evident with The Dreamers.

We were all rehearsing at someone's house with Easy Mersey, having real fun. In the middle of the jam we stopped playing because there was a street rumble going on outside. I peeped through the window and saw boys hitting people and shouting at each other. My ears went deaf. I lose my hearing when witnessing violence.

After that prolonged jam my voice went hoarse. At that time, I did not know how to take care of my voice. Often, I'd lose it after a long practice. Hola, we were scheduled to participate in a Concert At The Park gig in Manila, near the historic Luneta where the country's national hero Jose Rizal was executed. I went home that Saturday night feeling sick.

I performed at the gig the following day incapable of singing. I was relegated to just bass playing and that's a no-no. You have to play an instrument and sing back-up, at least. When I look back at my pictures taken that day, which I kept in some physical photo albums, I could still see the silent frustration I was feeling that day.

Adding insult to injury, our guitarist Michael and I arrived late. Of the five songs we were set to play, three featured a different bass player and lead guitarist, borrowed from either The Wall or Easy Mersey. Chris was mad at us. I was mad at myself. I have never been late for a gig after that incident.

Another point of tension was Jay Flores' departure in the early incarnation of our band. There will always be an odd guy in a pool of creatives. Sometimes the strange fellow stands out. In my experience, I haven't met anyone like Jay Flores. He's eccentric, weird, unpredictable, out of this world, and, to some extent, out of his mind.

Chris would open 'Lumipas Na Eksena' with '*Ayoko nang makinig sa'yo / Ang sabi mo mali kami*' (I don't want to listen to you / You said we were wrong). He was referring to Jay's transformation into a religious zealot. In those days it happened almost overnight. Suddenly, Jay became an expert on the bible and would fill our conversations of holy verses. Somewhere in the time we were rehearsing our first compositions and demos, Jay found God!

One day, Jay's rock 'n' roll anecdotes became passages and tales taken from the bible. Chris and I found it hard to react when he said that we were making music that won't save our souls.

Well, we were practically kids just trying to enjoy our youth, talking about guitars and girls, and the fun of being in a band. We saw Jay as a senior, ahead of us in terms of experience and of being a beatnik. But in a snap, he changed, and we had to charge on without him. I wrote this line about Jay. '*Samahan mo naman ako / Muli tayong maglalaro*' (Be with me and we will play together again).

Years later when Jay reappeared in my life and he became an addition to Syato, that line turned out to be fittingly meaningful. Jay did come back to play with me!

Chapter 12

In Excess

Almost every movie about rock bands, either based on a real life or fictitious, or a combo of both, portrays groups indulging in booze, sex, and name-it mischief. It's arguably cooler to party after a gig than have a prayer meeting. Weird but somehow it adds up when a rock star who's admired and emulated by fans throws furniture off the window of his hotel room.

I do understand that rock, or mere noise to those who really can't play the genre, could attract an unrighteous crowd. Wild sex is great to a rocker wannabe, which puts a premium on getting laid. You can be the least attractive person in the group, but if you have the character to command the stage, with a voice as manly as that singer from the band Creed, it's pussy galore!

But all this is no excuse to engage in debauchery.

I was fortunate not to be exposed to that kind of scene. The Dreamers tagged along with Free Souls, a band whose members claimed themselves as 'peacenik babies'. Chris was close to the members of Easy Mersey Band, a trio of odd-looking fellows you wouldn't think could punch a prick or steal a groupie from another band.

Back in the day with The Dreamers, seldom did we have drunken nights. When it comes to girls, self-confidence often derails me. I felt like I acted awkward all throughout my high

school and college days. Imagine a nerd trying to look cool. That
was me. Whereas Chris appeared to be a typical main man, and it
was no surprise that girls watching us would find him attractive,
I was his clumsy sidekick.

One time Chris and I got invited to some place by a classmate
of mine in Pol. Sci. class named Cooper. We were expecting to be
offered with some liquor as the guy was the type who'd want to
get drunk.

One morning in our class, Cooper wasn't himself. He was
acting erratically, like mumbling something while seated at the
back of the class. I thought he was drunk.

That evening, with Chris and I being his guests, I realized
that he was probably more than drunk when he pulled out a
marijuana joint, and asked us two to smoke with him. I already
had experience smoking one—my first time out of curiosity
and peer pressure during a debut party of another classmate. So,
I knew what to expect. As far as I knew, smoking it would make
me feel sleepy, or provide me some relaxed sensation.

Chris got excited by the idea of us smoking inside a
bathroom with the lights off. We did, then we chatted in the
living room after we were done. Perhaps I was not smoking it in
the proper way as I didn't experience its mind-altering effects.

Chris certainly went tripping that night. On our way home
when we boarded a jeepney, the famed Filipino public transport
vehicle, he started acting strangely. He held my arm tight, like he
needed me to watch over him.

'*Gel, lahat ng bagay lumalaki!*' (Gel, all things around us appear
to be bigger!), he whispered to me in a bewildered tone.

I thought he was joking. He wasn't. He said there was some
flying saucer somewhere in the distance. I wanted to laugh at
how he was reacting. But at the same time I was worried that his
behaviour would land us in trouble.

I just couldn't remember if it was my place or his. But we eventually got home safely. We didn't bump into any police officer or anyone we were not supposed to be interacting with during that commute.

Days later I told Chris I wish I had experienced what he had during that night. If I had seen the images he saw, like glowing lights and small things expanding, I would have sat down and wrote a song about it.

Ultimately, we never smoked a marijuana joint, nor any drug, again. Chris got scared about the experience. He said we didn't need it to be creative. I agree. We only needed each other's encouragement to write songs, alone or together.

Chris-Yugel, songwriting partners

Chapter 13

Fitting In

Some guys have all the *lack*! I feel I'm among them, one too many times I fell short because there's something lacking, whether in promotion of a song, the quality of its recording, or the skill set of either my bandmates or me. In Filipino parlance, *banderang kapus*.

When finding a mate to play music with, my instinct in determining who should be in the band depends on human connection. If we can talk about music and are agreeing on a lot of things, that's a good start.

There was this guy who got into The Dreamers to replace Jay Flores as guitarist. He had the talent and the aura. Chris met him at the time he was reaching out to all sorts of good-looking and could play–people to beef up our roster. It was college time; Chris was relatively a campus heart-throb. Another physically appealing boy in the group should spell a lot of difference.

While my post in The Dreamers could never be threatened by virtue of my co-founder status in the band, I was struggling to belong in our freshman college class, 1A2. I was in essence the weakest link among our set of friends or *barkada* in Filipino. I might have been too hard on myself but really, I felt like the nerd in a pool of cool boys and hot girls. I would laugh at anyone's jokes. I had to crack one very effective for anyone to bother to giggle. I had to befriend the loud, the beautiful, the bully-types, so I could win their trust and be on their side. I think I passed the test though. I'm still friends with most of them.

Chris and I were amused by this boy with a really bright character, who could play various instruments, sing, and write songs too. He had the look, with his confidence beaming and his neatly pressed hair asserting he wasn't inferior to anyone. We'd rather have someone with strong appeal than a boy looking like one of the roadies. In the Philippines, that is derogatory. The roadie carries the amplifiers and drives the van to bring the band to the gig venue.

At the time, our lead guitarist, Mike Dizon, who came on board prior to Mike Alforte, seemed a perfect fit for us with his wacky personality. We were serious boys, so he instantly became the clown. That fourth guy would have completed the line up, but he was too strong a presence. Sooner rather than later, we thought, he would clash with us over a melody or lyric line. He was a threat even to Chris' position as the acknowledged front man.

In hindsight, there was real potential if only we allowed their tandem to develop. I am certain then there would be friction among us three and I would land in an uncomfortable situation. Our Chris and Yugel tandem could only work if the other two in the band would play backup. Thus, having Mike—and Val later on—really made sense. Again, it was quite an immature move not to have another strong character in the band. That boy could have been the missing piece in the puzzle. We let him go. But not after some laughable sequence.

With Paolo, his first name, on board with us doing the demo of 'Lumipas Na Eksena', I had a laugh with Chris watching him showing off in front of us. His apparent versatility went off the mark when he volunteered to put a third voice to harmonize in the chorus.

To our surprise, Paolo was singing on a very low note. He totally missed it. His voice sounded like a giant man wanting to sing along with two dwarfs. He was ridiculously off. His voice was ruining the drama of our first full-on collaboration as songwriters. However, we couldn't right away say that it wasn't working.

Paulo may have a deeper knowledge about recording, but it showed he had a problem with how he would fit in. In a group you have to find your place. It's not just about showing others that you can do this and that.

Eventually we all just laughed, and we had his part cut out. That was the signal that he needed to go. He was a good-natured boy and should have contributed a lot to benefit our group, but The Dreamers couldn't be his band.

Chapter 14

The End of The Dreamers

Technically, The Dreamers released proper recordings that can be accessed thanks to digital music streaming. There are a total of six songs credited to our band, though it really didn't feature all four of us, but just Chris and me. My participation was much smaller compared to that of Chris. I submitted three compositions, played guitar on one of these songs, and reluctantly sung on one.

The album is a Various Artists compilation called *Anak Ng Edsa*, released in 2001, the year we disbanded.

Early that year, Chris pulled me into an album project to be produced by an acquaintance. I was enticed by the possibility that it could be our breakthrough. We'd been asked to give some of our compositions and record them under the supervision of the producer who had a home studio and was into digital music recording at a time when it was relatively new. We were to be credited as The Dreamers. I agreed.

But right on the get-go there were telltale signs that things were not right. First, we were not allowed to involve the other two Dreamers—Mike and Val. We were told that the drum tracks and even the bass could be handled by digital programming, while Chris could take on the guitar duties.

Second, on my first night joining the recording sessions, I quickly received some disparaging comments about my singing when they asked me to give a take on one of the compositions. I didn't expect a rude welcome. It seemed like the producer and another singer—who was there apparently to record other songs for the compilation—were ready to critique me. I wished they had instead encouraged me to fine-tune my singing. It was an uncomfortable night and it signalled how I would feel about the whole thing.

I didn't like the political tone of the project either. EDSA 2, the people power uprising that toppled the presidency of actor-turned-politician Joseph Estrada, was still fresh and the concept was that the songs should be against the perceived elitists—who in the mind of the producer manipulated the masses to wrest power from Estrada, long known as a man of the masses.

Yes, in the Philippines, the revolution that forced former dictator Ferdinand Marcos, who ruled the nation for twenty years, into exile had a sequel of sorts, just fifteen years after the events of EDSA Revolution in 1986. I may have been a political science student, but I didn't wish to write songs mainly for the purpose of producing tracks that espoused political statements.

One tune I wrote and really liked had its lyrics about friendship altered to pay honour to an activist. I had to write a line that goes 'Huwag nang hayaang bumalik sa EDSA' (Don't let us go back to EDSA) to suit the tone of the project. EDSA is a euphemism for fighting against tyranny. It's a strange line to say for a hater of tyrants, and for someone who majored in Political Science.

Another memorable evening involved a celebrity figure who visited the producer as we were having recording sessions. Sometime during this fateful visit, when Chris and I joined them in another room, a joint was passed around. In an instant the recording had become a different session! I wasn't sure how we begged off from becoming part of the rotation. But what I won't forget was when at some point a handgun was pulled out. The move wasn't really to signal that everybody in the room should take a puff. I just recall going home that night a bit shaken. Guitars and guns shouldn't be mixed.

Why I didn't back out early on was partly because I didn't want to leave Chris hanging. He was having a great time doing the album project. He was a key contributor. His compositions, his playing, his singing, were all praised by the producer and whoever comes in during the sessions. The Chris-Yugel tandem practically ended while Chris was at the peak of his creativity.

One time we were asked by the producer to come up with a song with certain requirements. Chris excused himself and I saw him working with his guitar. I knew he was trying to produce what was being asked. Why he didn't ask for my help—as there were moments we would sit down and see eye to eye while writing—was a puzzle. I didn't ask why. Later in life, when I looked back at that odd moment, I concluded that Chris was perhaps encouraged by the producer to work on his own as a reflection of his confidence in him. I was not seen as an equal.

When the album was released on CD, we were credited separately, not as Chris-Yugel. One of the songs I wrote, 'Halina't Sumama' (Come and Join), was even wrongly credited to Chris. I couldn't recall signing a document related to the release of the album. I just saw a copy out in the market, by surprise.

Obviously, because of the circumstances surrounding the creation of the compilation, I didn't rejoice seeing the *Anak Ng Edsa* CD even with The Dreamers name on it. It reminded me of an episode that disintegrated a partnership that was dear to me and a band I had hoped would make a name for ourselves.

The next time I would see Chris after *Anak Ng Edsa* was years later in another studio, not inside a home but in a facility. I was in a recording session sanctioned by an established music label, with my new band Syato. He was visiting the studio for something related to his also-new group.

I wasn't really angry with the producer whose name I would prefer not to mention. It was part of his character to be frank, and in all fairness, he was truly talented. He produced using his technical expertise right inside his home. In fact, when I learned that he was the one who remixed U2's 'With or Without You' so it would run well with the drum track from Tears For Fears' 'Shout', I bowed my head in acknowledgment. Years passing by made me feel thankful that he gave us that break to appear on a compilation album he had conceptualized.

This producer eventually became known as an audio expert, and I could only agree. He was a digital recording master long before many Filipino musicians followed suit.

If Chris and I could turn back time, I think we would probably wait for a few more years for that break that would put our band in the thick of things. The rock scene explosion in the music scene that began sometime in 2004 was coming and The Dreamers could have had a spot in an avalanche of bands that came out in the period.

But Chris and I were just too young to read the signs and too inexperienced to decide on what was good or not for our band.

The two other band members Val and Mike didn't say anything about the *Anak Ng Edsa* recording sessions. In October of 2001, we still played together in a John Lennon tribute gig featuring no-name Filipino bands playing for free. After that gig, Mike formally quit the group. He approached us and said it's time for him to focus on other things. Val didn't urge us to continue either. We never played as The Dreamers again after that gig.

For all that was dark with regards to *Anak Ng Edsa*, personally I see the light when I listen to 'Halina't Sumama'. Chris, who sung the track I penned—the one that was miscredited to him— may not agree but it is the one song in the compilation that sounds, even lyrically, like it does not want to be boxed within the compilation's concept and tone. I wish people would discover this record specifically because it sounds like The Dreamers, the four of us—and even those who had come to jam with us for a while—urging everyone to come and join in something that's fun.

'*Buksan ang isipan kung nakasara / Lawakan ang diwang nawawala dahil sa pagsibol ng mga dahong lanta na*' (Open the mind if it's closed / Widen the awareness being lost to withered leaves), its refrain lyrics say.

It's an invitation to gather as one and live for a cause. That was what we wanted as a group. We had a dream. Even if reality eventually woke us up in a bitter way. We had sweet memories that our minds and hearts can go back to. This song makes me relive the dream.

Refrain: Syato

Yugel Losorata after one of his interviews with a subject to write about (Photo by Ariel Obera)

Chapter 1

Office Band

It took around three months for me to put up a new band after the dissolution of The Dreamers. It was a quick rebound—and this was not because I wanted to prove to myself that I could do it without Chris Datijan. Things just fell into place.

As I was finishing my probationary period as an account executive for *Manila Bulletin*, I was transferred to its editorial section in September of 2000. Its head, Millie Vera, a brainy soft-spoken lady who later became a *ninang* (godmother) in my wedding, pulled me in after a mass resignation of her writers. She believed I could be trained. I knew I had the passion for writing, and could learn the ins and outs of journalism with experience and her mentorship.

A few months later after I had taken numerous writing assignments and delivered them day in and out, Ma'am Millie handed me a copy of an article I wrote about the Filipino basketball legend Robert Jaworksi, who I interviewed in person in his senate office. She had it edited with a remark that said the words 'very good'. It felt like I had passed the test. From then on, I've considered myself a professional writer blessed with a byline.

One morning inside the *Manila Bulletin* office in Intramuros, Manila, I was seated next to Joseph Gonzales, a guy oozing with confidence despite his small frame. He consistently made me laugh with clever jokes during our many conversations as co-writers for the supplement features. I must say we immediately developed a friendship as we were both into music and songwriting. In Manila it's ordinary to meet someone who can sing well. We are a nation of singers. But it's not every day there's a tunesmith next to you.

In that corner of the office that Monday, we were in front of our desktops writing articles we needed to produce for the newspaper when I suddenly said to him, 'Seph, I've heard from someone that they have a band in *Inquirer*. How about we form one ourselves?'

Joseph laughed, then he paused. 'Are you serious? Aren't you in a band already?'

Both the *Philippine Daily Inquirer* and *Manila Bulletin* were among the top three in the country in terms of sales and relevance. Still we thought it would sound cheap if we put a band for the purpose of just competing with another paper's band. We wanted to have a band that wrote and recorded its own songs.

I felt the idea could fly because Joseph had a deep friendship with Ronald Jayme, the other writer in our section. He got hired by the *Bulletin* before us. If Joseph could play guitar and write songs, Ronald could sing. Joseph told me that forming a band would make sense if we pull in RJ—that's Ronald's nickname in the office.

Joseph said, 'RJ's got a big voice, like that of Medwin Marfil of True Faith. I'll ask him to join.'

'Let me help you in convincing him,' I said.

Joseph was right about the Medwin comparison. When we later demoed our first three original songs and let friends hear them, most of them would say we sounded like True Faith, one of the hit-making Filipino bands that made it in the '90s.

When RJ committed to being the band's lead vocalist, it felt like the universe was conspiring with us. How in the world would three guys, all into music, find themselves in the same office, in the same department, and practically seatmates?

'What's the plan?' RJ asked in one of our lunches together.

'Yugel and I will write songs. You will sing them,' Joseph said.

'And we will play together. You on lead vocals, Joseph on guitar, me on bass, and we will do back-up singing,' I added.

'But we don't have a drummer. Don't we need to get one from somewhere?' RJ wondered.

Enter Mike Santos. Mike worked for *Bullletin*'s credit and collection department, just across where we were stationed. I met him prior to me floating the idea of creating a band

We met inside the ground floor restroom, literally while peeing. I found out he's into music too and that he played the drums for a band.

We were both facing the wall answering nature's call when I popped the question.

'Would it be cool to inform people that we met and decided to be bandmates in a restroom?' I quipped.

'There's logic to that. People sing in the bathrooms. It's like we found each other singing,' Mike said with a loud laugh. He has the loudest laugh, like he's giving it his all each time.

We didn't have to sing actually. We'd be the band's rhythm section. All we needed to do was make sure his drum kick went well with my groove.

When I introduced Mike to RJ and Joseph, they were amused to know there's a drummer in the same building welcoming the idea. It was decided he would join our band.

During our first jam in a rehearsal studio at SM Manila, the nearest branch of the country's biggest mall chain, we all got a good laugh each time we were able to finish a song without going off the rails. I would partly credit that to Mike and me being steady. One moment, when Joseph stopped playing to fix something on his guitar, we just kept going and RJ continued singing. I knew from watching The Beatles famously playing on the roof that it was all right to do this, just like when Paul McCartney and Ringo Starr kept the beat and groove going, even when the guitar amplifiers had been turned off.

The Dreamers disbanded in late 2001. By early 2002, I was in a new band. By being officemates, we four members were all decidedly both—creative and professional. We were also older and wiser than four college friends still deciding on what work to do after graduation.

One day, after continuous days of overtime work. RJ, Joseph, and I found our names printed in the staff box of a special feature fold. As we needed a band name, we agreed on the name Staffbox.

Chapter 2

Songwriting at Work

I didn't set out to form a band when I entered *Manila Bulletin* as an employee in the summer of 2000.

But I was thrusted by fate right where new bandmates were waiting. I doubted at first if working with a new songwriter partner was the best move as I was still grasping for breath from the stress of dropping The Dreamers from my life.

My mind cleared up when I heard Joseph's composition 'Lubusan'. *Time to open a new chapter*, I thought. I was amazed by the catchy tune and sincere lyrics. I couldn't resist contributing so I helped out in the arrangement. I suggested that the bass and drums should come after the first verse.

When Joseph asked what could possibly be the best title for it, I said it's obvious it should be called 'Lubusan' because it is the last word in the chorus and it's a strong word. I made that suggestion sounding like it's straight from the songwriters' playbook.

We demoed the track and put it as the lead piece in our three-song Staffbox demo CD, which also included 'Stop the World', a song I created right after the disbandment of The Dreamers and which I took as an inspired piece of work believing that it's time to move on and progress. The third song was 'Himig', a collaborative composition between Joseph and me where I had to supply a chorus after hearing a verse and an unfinished pre-chorus. The process reminded me of what Chris and I employed in 'Lumipas Na Eksena'.

The demo was submitted to Ivory Music & Video by my friend Jhi Gopez, a band manager whose production gig 'Feminine Force' I wrote about in *Manila Bulletin*. The demo landed on the desk of Snaffu Rigor, Ivory's A&R (Artist & Repertoire) at that time. He heard it and then signed us.

In one special jamming session with Mr Rigor—whose brother Spanky was a member of VST & Co., which was a band associated with the Manila Sound of the '70s—said that he thought our sound was highly influenced by VST & Co. and he suggested changing our name to Syato. We all knew that Syato is a traditional street game in the Philippines involving two sticks, to be played by a hitter and a catcher.

At that time there was a lady politician in regular news rotation with the surname Chato, which sounded like Syato. I initially thought it was a bit off for a name, and wanted to ask Sir Snaff if he could think of another one. Good thing I didn't do it as that may have appeared like I was being pushy with a producer who's signing our band; he may find it off-putting. We unanimously agreed on Syato.

Our song 'Lubusan' was initially slated to be our lead single, which eventually opened the Syato debut album. All of us believed in it being the strongest cut, including our decorated producer who had scored numerous hits as a songwriter himself. Alas, it was bumped off by another composition by Joseph, called 'Kailanman', which became the actual lead single.

Years prior, I had found Chris as we were developing as teenage songwriters. Joseph, six years older than me, was a full-fledged tunesmith. In one of our office chats, he showed me a little poem book containing his poetry. It's always an honour to be collaborating with someone who's more talented. The fact that

I was feeling more confident and still understood the greatness of Joseph's work as a songwriter meant Joseph was on a truly different level.

In one of our subsequent TV interviews, I joked that Joseph was older than me by sixteen years! It was my way of showing him how I look up to him. If I turned out to be flying on a magic carpet, Joseph got on board a flying saucer!

Ivory Music & Video gave us a recording contract, which included publishing our first official album as a band. We only had ten song slots and we were set to record in March of 2005. We got to work.

While Joseph and I wrote some songs separately, we were hell-bent on forming a songwriting partnership. We thought that would give us extra credibility as a team of musicians, and on a personal note, it was a bit of a nod to the Chris-Yugel tandem. In the end, we were able to work on four songs together. There were three more that we did, but the band failed to rehearse them enough in time for recording.

Of the four, 'Himig' was the most special for us because it encapsulated our love for music. We wrote it inside the *Manila Bulletin* premises at midnight while having a break from overtime work.

We were working on a Mother's Day special supplement project that consisted of articles related to motherhood, which we wrote and curated. Work on such a fold tends to extend to the wee hours and there would be an intermittent lull where we would chat or compose. There was a guitar kept in one of the cabinets so we took it out and I played the chorus I had in mind.

I started writing a song called 'Sayo Lang' as a paean to my affection for my girlfriend-officemate Kaye Villagomez. Kaye was a writer from the Entertainment section of *Manila Bulletin*. She is the love of my life and became my wife. We were married at the Manila Cathedral.

I had chosen 'Sayo Lang' to be our wedding song, and RJ sang it live, accompanied by the church pianist. *'Ilang taon ko nang hinihintay dumating ang isang katulad mo sa buhay ko'* (For years I've been waiting for someone like you), says the opening line.

I usually don't encounter problems when writing choruses and stanzas. Trouble often comes with how to meld them. Joseph came to the rescue. His bit, a couplet, really turned the song around. It was a pre-chorus that I didn't think I would be able to top, at least for what was necessary for the song. Every time I hear it, it puts a smile on my face that my buddy exerted his best in making a song largely mine worthy of his contribution. Kaye was walking down the grand aisle of the historic church as the song that had yet to be properly recorded reverberated through its walls.

My collaboration with Joseph was more impactful than what I had with Chris before. Our partnership produced ten songs good for a full-length album in CD format released by a record label that already signed a roster of hitmakers prior to us.

Chapter 3

Signing with Snaffu

This is a moment I love replaying in my mind over and over. For weeks I was waiting for a call from a record producer, the person who'd oversee the recording sessions for our single or album. That man was Snaffu Rigor—someone old school but accomplished. He had the power to sign us up or say we didn't pass the audition—the one we would give inside the recording studio of Ivory Records called Greenhills Sound, located in San Juan City.

During the audition, we played five songs, mostly our compositions. It was nerve-wracking having to do it in front of Mr Rigor whose track record included writing the hit songs 'T.L. Ako Sa'yo' and 'Bulag, Pipi, At Bingi'.

Syato had been rehearsing and doing a few gigs for a couple of years prior to the moment so we were kind of prepared. After the session I felt confident we were going to pass it, but I needed to formally hear it from Sir Snaffu. The waiting game began when he told us they were going to assess us first.

Interestingly, we had already had a session at the same studio when we produced the first Syato demo in 2003 under the supervision of the same mixing engineer, Joel Mendoza, who had helped deliver hit albums in the past, including those from April

Boy Regino, a successful Filipino balladeer famous for wearing the Chicago Bulls cap in his public performances.

Sir Snaffu cracked a nice joke when he confronted Joel about not informing him that he already encountered us before. One of the stalwarts of Manila Sound that was popular in the late '70s and '80s said in jest, 'Joel, how dare you not inform us you've already heard the music of Syato?!'

Joel just smiled. He didn't have to answer.

I was with Kaye at a park in Makati City facing the Glorietta Mall when that call came and I heard exactly what I wanted to hear. Snaffu Rigor informed me that Ivory Music had greenlit the signing of our band Syato. We'd soon record our debut album!

That day in 2004 has been etched in my memory. I was walking to and fro frantically as I was talking to Sir Snaff—dropping the letter 'u' sounded cooler sometimes.

According to Kaye, I had a smile on my face that reflected the good news. I could also imagine Sir Snaffu's face looking glad, knowing he was making someone extremely happy. It was a dream come true for me, and for the rest of the band who I immediately informed and who had to pinch themselves just thinking about the possibilities of being a signed recording artist.

Struggling musicians who have been playing their originals in small bars, with more than half of the people watching them also their own friends, and who are not used to getting paid at all, know what a record contract means. Established recording acts would ask for contract details to see how they would benefit, especially in the long run. For indies with nearly zero hope of getting signed, just being handed a record contract meant the world. The girl of your dreams is now sitting on your lap!

The meaning of that call goes beyond just being really lucky. It's about seeing the light at the end of a long tunnel.

I tried not to cry in front of Kaye as it would look embarrassing. We were a few months away from getting married. I was conscious not to show emotional vulnerability. You shouldn't cry because of a recording contract.

Kaye, however, knew what that meant to me. Every once in a while, when we would pass over that park, we'd be reminded of that moment—the respected hitmaker calling, the dreamer's face glowing.

When the actual signing happened weeks later, I savoured the moment with RJ, Joseph, and Mike; all of us feeling like we made it. Our band Syato was an unlikely signee. We were all short-haired, office working guys looking like we were off to some child's christening. Very formal and normal-looking fellows.

We had a picture showing us regular eight to fivers inside the boardroom of a popular record label with a renowned record producer and the label's big boss. That photo came out in the *Manila Bulletin* later, and I had the privilege of writing about the experience.

To some in our circle, our past time leading to a record contract was an accomplishment rarely realized. The triumph of being signed not only served as victory for a group of officemates synergizing their musical talents but, personally, I was morally boosted by the fact that somehow I had fulfilled the dream that Chris and I couldn't. I had to attribute it in some way to my never-say-die spirit, which I've been trying to live by since becoming a fan of the popular basketball team Barangay Ginebra. Jaworski popularized the mantra. That it's not over 'til it's over.

After recording the album throughout the summer of 2005, we looked ahead to promoting our self-titled debut.

We weren't able to pick the single of our choice as it was the leading FM station Love Radio that decided on it, in particular, station manager Willy Espinosa whose hunches were valued as the sound of a cash register by labels. Voila, 'Kailanman', his choice, did not become a hit!

A couple of friends did try to imply that the lyrics to 'Kailanman' were corny. Well, the chorus goes, *'Ikaw ay akin.*

Ako ay sayo / Tayo'y iisa / Laging magkasama' (You are mine / I am yours / We are one / Always together). At that time, I wouldn't have asked Joseph to change the words as I trusted my songwriting pal too much. I did prefer his original English lyrics for the song, which he'd titled 'You're My You'.

Fatedly, we were obliged to do an all-Tagalog album because we were being positioned as Manila Sound–influenced. That was fine and we were willing to oblige. So 'Stop the World' had to be set aside, too, while 'You're My You' became 'Kailanman'.

Later when reminiscing about Syato's first years, I felt we should have written better lyrics for the carrier single. In a perfect world, we could have asked Sir Willy to pick the single-material from our demos so we'd know which track to give more careful treatment to.

Signing a record contract is also losing some creative control. Who'd care about that when you're signing one for the first time? We were just happy to be out with an album of our own and to hear our music being played on the radio. Yes, it would have been a better move if we released an upbeat track instead of 'Kailanman', a ballad that does not really showcase our band's sound, or to be specific, the rest of the album. It's the slowest in tempo among the songs and the only one that didn't feature drums. The picking of the first single was really beyond our control.

I received another phone call prior to the album's release. It was from MG Mozo, the Ivory label's lady executive who's also the daughter of top honcho Tony Ocampo—whom we met on signing day and was a typical image of a veteran record label head. The message from her was clear. 'Kailanman' would be released as the lead single.

'*May problem ba tayo doon?*' (Do we have a problem with that?), she asked me.

Looking back, it was not right to insist on 'Lubusan', or 'Scorpio', the other upbeat song in contention as a lead single. The record label and the radio head should have known better.

Postscript: The Mozos became a family friend. In fact, I supported Ma'am MG's daughter, Sofia, when she was launched as a bossa nova performer. I played the bass guitar during her mall tour.

Original Syato lineup (from left) Joseph Gonzales, Yugel Losorata,
Ronald Jayme, Mike Santos, and Jay Flores

Chapter 4

Melody or Lyrics

I consider songwriting as perhaps the most important gift I have. Some people in my circle have praised my writing skills, sincerely expressing their admiration for the way I write, which I truly appreciate. However, there's something in songwriting that feels more magical to me. Whereas I need to develop my know-how in writing by reading and writing consistently, songwriting is like a built-in capability, one that just comes, even if I can't formally read music.

I'm an *ouido* like most Filipino musicians, but not everybody deciphering music by ear can write songs.

I feel that among the many songwriters, only few are gifted enough to write really good songs, regardless of whether these become hits or not. There's this rocking tune called 'Memories' recorded by an obscure Filipino band called Eyescream. Its strong melody and the simply effective 'I remember you forgetting me' line make my blood rush each time I hear the song. Yet, the song didn't reach mainstream listeners. I pity those who haven't heard it, in particular those convincing themselves that the latest well-promoted, badly written track of a famous band has good recall.

I have been a music critic in my own right so that's where I'm coming from. At a time when CDs were still the main format in releasing recordings, listening to other people's music and new songs were my routine. Most of the time I would do it because I needed to write about some new stuff. When CDs became obsolete in lieu of digital releases, I had collected more than enough to literally fill up a wall. Stacks of CDs from all kinds of artists adorn our living room, placed like piles of books on shelves.

One time my wife and I argued about which is more important, the melody or the lyrics. Of course, it's the marriage of the two that makes a good song. But for the sake of answering the question, I go for melody. Kaye's a lyrics person, always weighing in on a song based on the words the singer spits. I think that when you are a songwriter, you care about melodies more emphatically. I do think that some tunesmiths care less about it and invest more on the words at the risk of the song becoming more forgettable. Michael Jackson described effective songs as 'killer melodies'. He spent so much time working on his solo albums and even discarded several tracks—the melodically weak ones I suppose— to determine the finest cuts. 'Thriller' had only nine tracks. Seven of them hit the top 10 of the US Billboard Hot 100 chart.

Chapter 5

Bass Line Euphoria

In the summer of 2005, we formally began recording our album at Greenhills Sound Studio—a venue where great Filipino recordings took place, which Joel Mendoza—our veteran recording engineer—would constantly remind us about. 'We're on holy ground!' he would say. We felt like we were street children allowed to be in a play place for well-sheltered kids.

I was twenty-seven at the time and had just got married. It was certainly a fine way to spend the first months of my married life. I entered a formal recording studio after having my honeymoon in Bangkok where Kaye covered an international film festival. It was an inspiring period for me. I was on top of the world!

Such a vibe helped when I laid the bass lines for many of the songs on the album—less jitters, more confidence. Years of playing with Chris and The Dreamers and the practice of the pre-Syato days paid off.

There was one funny yet poignant moment I will never forget. Joel, being the seasoned studio guy he is, pointed out that my notes were rambling while playing the ballad 'Kailanman'. The song written by Joseph was initially an English piece with drums and was the first song we ever jammed to. He had to rewrite the words to fit our all-Filipino language album.

It would eventually be released as a single, with no drums at all. I felt sorry for Mike. He wouldn't be able to close his eyes to get into the groove with his foot on the kick. We joked that he was sleeping all the while we were recording 'Kailanman'.

I was being conscious as to provide a significant contribution to the piece because I didn't have a hand in the songwriting part. That seemed natural for people who write songs to step up somewhere when the situation relegates them to the role of a pure instrumentalist.

If you listen to the track, you'd hear the bass take centre stage while the singer is resting, and before the lead guitarist takes over. That happened because I took those notes from an old song I had written. So, my part had its own existence as a melody. It was the verse tune of a ballad I had written back in high school. Somehow the melody fitted Joseph's composition. It became a subtle bass solo.

At first, I thought I was wasting a whole song for a short bass passage to a track I hadn't even written. But I may have had a hunch that the piece would eventually be chosen as the album's carrier single so I needed to bring my A-game.

When Joel commented on my quite busy playing, Sir Snaffu cut him off and said in his inimitable smile, 'There was nothing wrong in the notes, Joel. *Ang tawag dyan talent.*' (That's called talent.)

I wanted to laugh but I kept it to myself and instead basked in muted euphoria.

Chapter 6

Out there for Bliss

The work inside the studio is as fulfilling as being at home and doing the things you want to do. As blissful as that, but on another level, is going out in front of people to showcase what you got.

I was certainly having the time of my life when we appeared in front of a live basketball crowd inside the Cuneta Astrodome in Pasig City. We were given the spotlight during the lull between the first and second game of a PBA double header. PBA is Philippine Basketball Association, the oldest professional cage league in Asia, and Philippines' local version of the NBA in the US.

As the set-up forced us to do lip-syncing, it was really just us in the flesh with our unplugged instruments, mimicking ourselves performing our upbeat song 'Scorpio'. The game ahead featured the league's most popular team so there was a considerable number of spectators to see us. Whether or not they were watching us or doing something else while we were on didn't really matter. It was a triumphant feeling just being there in centre court.

As a composer, it was pure joy knowing your song is being heard all over the venue.

I recalled shouting through the mic the chant for the popular basketball club Barangay Ginebra out of sheer jubilation. The team was set to play in the main game so we had the extra privilege of watching them after our guest performance. I think most of my bandmates went home after our performance. I stayed because I'm a true fan, both of the said team and the league.

The PBA gig was great even if your audience was primarily there to watch basketball. We later laughed at the thought of us pretending to be performing. Each of us was claiming to be the best actor, meaning, the most believable in trying to appear as if he's really playing or singing. I fully understand why some musicians hate lip syncing.

I would have loved to see my son, Ryde, see me perform for the PBA but he wasn't even born yet. Ryde as a toddler began watching PBA games live. Once or twice we went to watch games at the same venue where Syato performed. Too bad it was a one-off gig. I never got to do it with Ryde watching.

Appearing on PBA was proof—somewhat—you're part of the mainstream. You don't step on the hard court without some sort of credibility that you made it, or you belong. Years later I wrote a song I wish the PBA could use as a theme song, called 'Basketball Pinoy'. It was my ode to a league I am a fan of.

The much-later Syato personnel recorded the song fine. My old mate Michael Alforte from The Dreamers even contributed some guitar licks. It was Dex Facelo of Alamid who came up with the stirring guitar riff at the beginning of the track. I let him hear the composition and he sent me his idea of how the guitar may sound. For some reason I wasn't able to pull in Dex in the proper recording. When Michael came, I asked him if he could do what Dex suggested and he duly delivered.

Even a media guy could end up struggling with finding the proper connections to push a plan so the track remained unused by the league it paid tribute to. Perhaps one day someone from the PBA office would hear it and a young band would interpret it and earn a guest spot to perform it live. That will definitely be a personal victory. Here I am again being the king of wishful thinking!

Chapter 7

Scorpio on TV

Long after our ten-song album and its two singles were released and promoted by the Ivory label, Joseph—my Syato songwriting mate—felt nostalgic and he posted on social media a couple of shots of our band performing. One was a picture of us in action at the PBA and the other at a Sunday variety show. We actually appeared twice on national TV that summer of 2006, performing 'Scorpio', our second single.

For me, Joseph, RJ, and Mike, those were the highlight reels. From an idea on a Monday morning, our little group ended up on mainstream TV on two Sunday afternoons.

Speaking of 'Scorpio', the song is a Joseph-Yugel collaboration that closes out the album in an upbeat mode. Lyrically it is a track I started writing to touch on a subject I had a hard time dealing with—romantic jealousy, or being possessive over someone. At the time of writing, my would-be wife Kaye was my girlfriend and I couldn't stop myself from getting jealous whenever she was talking to another man, in particular, one of our co-workers in the supplements department.

In hindsight there was nothing wrong in Kaye talking to some guys, especially when she was in an office environment and professional interactions were happening. It was my character flaw that was to blame. I was young and didn't know better. And

Joseph and I being both born under the zodiac sign Scorpio felt that astrology had to do with that.

Scorpio men are thought to be among the most irrationally jealous guys. One of the lines I wrote, '*At walang pasabi'y magseselos / Patawad kung padalos-dalos*' (Without warning you will get jealous / Sorry if I'm being reckless), verbally pointed this out. Hence, we called the song 'Scorpio'.

One evening, we (members of the band) were together and jumped in jubilation when we found out that we landed on the sixteenth spot of a Top 20 MYX Pinoy countdown of Filipino-penned songs, as tallied by MYX channel. MYX is the Philippines' version of the globally renowned MTV channel. It was in a local sense a key indicator of how a song was faring in the public eye.

That accomplishment formally informed listeners that we're a full-on band, and that 'Kailanman' really didn't introduce our act exactly as it should.

With Joseph being the songwriter behind the first single 'Kailanman' that rotated on mainstream radio and was also backed with a music video under the watch of our record label, I felt glad I had co-written 'Scorpio', a personal track expressing sentiments of wicked jealousy and over-possessiveness in a pop, rock 'n' roll ditty. If you wonder if I somehow got jealous that it was Joseph's song that was picked for our first single, I won't really deny it!

The shows we appeared on to promote 'Scorpio' and virtually launch our band were top Sunday varieties: ABS-CBN's ASAP and GMA-7's SOP. Both ABS-CBN and GMA are the country's top major networks and were fierce rivals at the time.

For ASAP I remember we were on a round movable stage that was ushered into the audience's view after some voice over introduction about our band. Then once the performance began, adrenaline rush took over and I enjoyed every second of it. It was customary to have one of the hosts sing with a guest performer, so popular balladeer Erik Santos performed with us. He did say he liked the track during our little chat after the performance. He noted that he picked it because it sounded fun.

On the day of our guest appearance on SOP that came a couple of weeks after, I was oddly feeling not that okay because the night before, I had noticed that 'Scorpio' did not go up further on MYX countdown, and it was already slipping down. It peaked at number sixteen. That was it.

Our jubilation was thus short-lived as I felt broken for it not going higher. It was immature of me. Some bands couldn't even get to record their songs properly. For Christ's sake we were on a notable countdown and were being seen performing live on national TV!

While backstage at the GMA-7 studio I saw a familiar face beside an old man in a wheelchair. She was Angela Colmenares who had the distinction of being a classmate of mine in both college and elementary school. I was surprised to learn that she was the daughter of the man to be brought on stage and whose other daughter was the actress Angel Locsin. Up until that point, I didn't realize that Angela, who I knew as a quiet, shy girl who transformed into an outspoken activist during our Political Science class years, was the sister of a big-time celebrity. She was there escorting her father to appear on TV. We exchanged hellos.

Buoyed by my discovery, I suddenly realized Angela does look similar to Angel. I laughed at myself. How had I not see it before?

So much was happening that afternoon. The thrill of appearing on TV was running through my fingertips. Small wonder that the surprise of finding out Angela being the sister of one of the hottest girls in showbiz didn't really bother me.

Ultimately, our band's moment came like a flash. Quickly we were led to the stage to plug in our instruments, like a scene from a comedy film when images are forwarded to a rapid pace. Singer Ogie Alcasid, who was the host assigned to sing parts of the song, approached me to say hi. Kaye wrote about him in the *Manila Bulletin*, and she had introduced me to him prior to that guest stint.

Even though I actually couldn't hear the bass sound and was just playing the song by muscle memory, the performance went smoothly, and somebody captured the moment on a digital camera. I was at the far end of the picture. Joseph was closest to the camera. To be in the same shot performing with Ogie now feels like a once-in-a-lifetime moment you would be happy just to be in.

Chapter 8

Stitches and Bridges

Meeting Ogie Alcasid is bound to be great if you're into songwriting. He's a master balladeer who wrote some enduring Filipino love songs. And it was great. However, the fan boy in me went full throttle when I encountered singer-songwriter Per Sorensen of Fra Lippo Lippi, a Norwegian duo whose songs have been embraced by Filipinos.

I met one of my songwriting idols twice when I had to write about him being in Manila. By the time I was featuring musicians, I was already a freelance journalist covering music. The first interview was for *Manila Bulletin*, the second time for *Manila Standard*.

Per is the singer, keyboard player, and melodist of the group particularly famous among Filipinos during the 1980s. I'm puzzled why the rest of the world didn't find the group as worthy as our country did. Per's talent is a classic example of how melodies can turn simple words into a piece of work that won't leave your head. If you look at the chorus lyrics of their hits 'Angel' or 'Stitches and Burns', there's hardly any poetry in them. The singer's just saying he wishes to see a girl one more time or he doesn't want to see her any more. But then when these words are sung in the melody lines they were fitted in, the results are sublime.

I'm not taking away anything from lyricist and bassist Rune Kristofferson. He wrote 'Love Is a Lonely Harbour', which I really like. The point is, you can replace the lyrics with other words and the song will still stand owing to its strong melody. We're talking about decent alternative lyrics, not stupid ones that would make it comical, like the temporary lyrics of 'Scrambled Eggs' to the eventual most covered song of all time, 'Yesterday', by who else but Paul McCartney of The Beatles.

On both occasions I spoke to Per, he made it sound like melodies just came to him easily, at least until the need for a bridge would arise, and then he'd be stuck. That's where, as I see it, his genius comes in.

In our chat at the Hilton Hotel in Resorts World Manila in 2018, where each media invitee was given a slot to face him for a short interview, he noted while speaking about his fondness for a song's bridge, 'I take pride in writing good bridges. That's putting something else entirely different after the verses and chorus. It may be half groove or however you want it, but somehow not running on the same chords.'

He gave, as an example, the 'time after time' part in 'Stitches and Burns' wherein from chorus, the tempo changes and introduces a new melody run for two bars before it goes back to the familiar chorus.

After that press event where he performed 'Beauty and Madness' to a stunned Filipino press with just his powerful voice and his fingers smoothly caressing the keyboard, I met him at the hotel's poolside smoking area. I was surprised to find out that he smokes. We made some small talk before he showed me a kind of black chewing gum that he eats after smoking. That must be part of his secret, I thought.

While he naturally preferred the studio recording of 'Every time I See You', I personally think that the live version, which appears in a 'Best of' collection dated 2003, is better, especially the final choruses with his vocal ad lib. Often the live rendition won't be able to recapture the exact beauty of the master recording. But there are occasions when the performances have more emotions and are better-sung.

The Dreamers used to cover 'The Distance Between Us' during gigs and I would sing it myself. There were these jeepneys dubbed 'Nova-Blum' traversing the stretch from Novaliches, a municipality where I spent most of my youth, to Blumentritt, a key spot of PUV (Public Utility Vehicles) terminals in the city of Manila, and back. I used to hop on these jeepneys. Then transfer to ones that would pass UST. The drivers and their back riders usually beefed up their jeepneys with all sorts of accessories. To cap it off, they assembled a boosted sound system to make the sound trip on new wave music cerebral. Fra Lippo Lippi hits were shoo-ins on such a playlist.

Album cover of Syato's self-titled debut album produced and released in CD format by Ivory Music & Video in 2005. (Images taken by Ibarra Deri and Tess Puzon-Rivera)

Chapter 9

Revolu*tune* in the Head

A friend in college found it odd seeing me sing or speak to myself while walking around or sitting alone between classes in one of the pavilions facing the UST AB building. I wasn't being crazy. There must be a tune running inside my head that I needed to hum or put provisional lyrics to. It's a regular thing. It has been part of my being ever since I started writing songs.

I never forced it unless I was pressed by commissioned work. Often, I would sit down with a guitar and play chord combinations in the hope that I come across a decent melody line to begin a song with. I can't predict the moment when a tune would play out in my head. My classmate witnessed me in my songwriting mode. I can't blame him for thinking that it was weird to see me singing like I was talking to someone else.

Thanks to voice recorders on mobile phones. A tunesmith can easily put to tape what's in his head. Back in the '90s there were times when I'd spend a couple of hours humming a particular chorus-like tune, only to totally forget it after my attention was directed elsewhere. Scary to think that there could have been some hit tunes that slipped away because I didn't have a recorder to keep them.

Well, after years of struggling to score hit songs, I no longer worry about those lost tunes. I'd like to think they didn't stay in my head because they were not good enough to stick. A tune is beautiful if you put the lyrics of 'Butchikik'—by novelty legend Yoyoy Villame—to it. When you can sing a melody line with phrases like '*momo chichang*' and it doesn't make you laugh, boy you just caught a good tune.

For us in Syato, our debut album's crowning glory was a melody honouring songwriting and the power of music. When Joseph showed us a couple of verses he wrote, I challenged myself to write a melody and a passage fit for a chorus. I take pride in being able to do that. It's always easier to start a song than to come up with something that should fit an incomplete tune, let alone if the need is a chorus, which obviously should be more recallable than the stanzas or refrain.

When the album was released, Joseph informed us of hearing one of his nephews sing the chorus part. That made me smile. Some of my siblings liked this track of ours and a tribute video for my father was created by my niece, Bianca, after he passed away. The song was put to good use.

For 'Sa Ulan', which I wrote by myself, the melody struck me while I was recalling those days as a kid playing in the rain, just allowing the water from the sky to drop on my head, I see it more as a celebration of being alive and being in love—just like what I'm saying in the song. A former officemate who spent more than two decades of his life serving the *Manila Bulletin* as an ad taker said he had taken the track to heart. On the bed by myself playing guitar, I felt good singing 'Sa Ulan' after I was done writing. In my alternative reality, this track is evoking good vibes for a lot of people, remembering days when they basked in the innocence and the sheer joy of a simple life.

Chapter 10

Just Put It on Record

One reason I fear death is the thought of dying with songs still in my chest. Ones that have yet to be recorded and released. I can't take them with me into oblivion.

In songwriting, it's regrettable when you miss recording a strong melody running in your head or forget to jot down a clever lyric on paper. Completing a composition is a work of art, but unless you have it recorded for posterity, and put it out there so it exists even after you leave the face of the Earth, the song becomes nothing but a melody you once created out of thin air but failed to keep.

You can't really ever be sure if there's anyone who is willing to spare around four minutes on your music—to listen to the song you wrote pouring out your heart. What matters though is making your work available for anyone interested in listening to it.

Believe me, I'm not making much money from songwriting. A majority of Filipino songwriters don't make much money. No wonder people tell us to get a real job instead. Yet, I feel some pressure to formally record most of my fleshed-out compositions. I see it as one of my life's main purposes—it's why I am here breathing and why I want to live a long life. It may not be as important as my obligation to do what I can to help my son, Ryde, achieve his aim of becoming a professional basketball player or whatever else he wants to do in adulthood, but nevertheless I feel a responsibility to make sure my tunes get recorded.

Speaking from experience, you can't predict when inspiration will arrive. It's an edge if you always have an instrument with you. Tinkering with a set of family chords may trigger the birth of a melodic line. In some instances, it might happen in unexpected places, like the chorus to Syato's 'Ayoko Na', which came while I was about to walk up the stairs of an MRT train station.

Smartphones have provided us with recording apps for the tunes we hum. The feeling you get knowing you have recorded your latest melody is bliss. It's like finding a thousand-peso bill on the floor and picking it up without guilt because you don't know to whom it belongs.

It's magical when I get to improvise a bass line or an ad lib instrumental part, or a vocal style that enhances the melody, and then by luck somebody presses the recording button.

Years later a former officemate from *CNN Philippines*—where I worked as a copy editor for some time—sent me his composition, requesting if I could give it a listen. I found him appreciative of my identity as a musical artist, so I did and was surprised to find out he'd written a good one. I felt excited by it and realized the track needed a bridge. Per Sorensen would agree. The verse and chorus of my mate's composition are like siamese twins, and they needed a reliable cousin.

Without really forcing it, a tune that sounded like a good detour from the available melody of a song Eddy, my co-news script editor, liked to call 'Mirrors' came over my head. Immediately I recorded it on my phone, went to the keyboard and polished it. If for some reason I forgot to record it, Eddy and I would have lost the opportunity to collaborate. The sudden closure of *CNN Philippines*, which happened before he reached out to me, made our efforts to team up as composers more poignant.

Chapter 11

Camping and Humming

By the time I attended the first FILSCAP (Filipino Society of Composers, Authors, and Publishers) Songwriting camp in 2016, I was way beyond being a novice writer. My experience in songwriting has its roots in high school. I started with mere melodies and poetry. Back then, I couldn't accompany the words with chords.

Then through experience and self-learning I began discovering what family chords would embrace what melody. It came naturally. I guess we people who are not formally trained but can make music anyway have no clear explanation other than we have the ears and voice that translate emotions into music.

That songwriting camp was more of a venue where we could expand our network in the field. I don't think any of the attendees were there to start from scratch. Frankly speaking we're all scratched souls looking for kindred spirits and we found each other in that pretty place just outside Metro Manila. I got to spend time with people who think like me.

There were four celebrity mentors that weekend and I was assigned to one called Camp Mariposa, anchored by singer-songwriter Ebe Dancel of Sugarfree fame. 'Mariposa' is one of his band's hits from their debut album that introduced his songwriting skill and high-pitched vocals.

While it's easy to be starstruck when in the same room with a celebrity, my profession as an entertainment journalist gave me room to develop a mindset that these hailed artists are not that different from regular people. They are just fortunate to score a hit or two and be counted as public figures. It could be anyone from the regular pool of songwriters who are equally talented but just couldn't get the break. That's not taking away anything from Ebe. He's an inspiring figure and for me he's among the finest who made it. You can check his band's other classics—'Hari Ng Sablay', 'Tulog Na', 'Telepono', 'Burnout', and 'Huwag Ka Nang Umiyak'.

I had interviewed and written about Sugarfree a number of times. Thus, Ebe easily recognized me when it was my time to enter his room to show what I had composed in the time he'd given us. To be honest, there was some kind of bitterness in me that I had to see him as if I was auditioning my piece when I was used to throwing questions myself for him to answer. It would have been better if we were in the same room collaborating on a song!

Not being easily starstruck has its drawbacks and it made me think I deserved to be an equal instead of being mentored. At first I felt uncomfortable with the situation but no one had forced me to join that Camp in the first place. I wasn't intimidated by Ebe because I knew I have a couple of compositions in my vault that can sit side by side with his famous songs. Call it guts. I must say I am proud of my babies.

Funny, as it turned out, when my moment with Ebe came, I was humbled. When he asked me to check if the guitar in my arms was perfectly tuned, it gave me the impression that he was a professional who won't settle for mediocrity or anything less than precise. When I was singing the composition I wrote to him, which I called 'Menopausa', a word play I thought was a comical reference to 'Mariposa', he asked me to stop and said that a particular melody line didn't fit the chord I strummed. He was that sharp!

My singing could be a culprit anytime of the day and he caught me barefooted. I regretted not being able to come up with a stronger tune for him to hear. I would have wanted to showcase a composition I wrote called 'Sangandaan', which was partly inspired by his style. However, the tune for 'Menopausa' was the one in my head at the time. I wish I had offered a stronger composition. I wasn't surprised when Ebe didn't pick my piece as among the top three compositions from his pool of campers.

Well, he picked one written by singer-actor Mark Bautista titled 'Beto-beto'. It was a novelty piece with easy recall and was loaded with punchlines. It was something composers with a serious demeanour wouldn't dare write.

Arguably, Mark's piece was chosen partly because of his status as a celebrity himself, a matinee idol at that. If I was in Ebe's shoes, I wouldn't have picked it. But in all fairness, Mark was cool and down-to-earth, never ever making others feel like he was above them because of his fame.

In July 2019, I wrote in my music column—published by *Manila Standard*—my recollection of that weekend at a facility in Antipolo City in the province of Rizal. I said that 'somehow you'd feel it was necessary to be in such a spot as validation of your lifelong passion.' Dex Facelo, who wrote the band Alamid's classic 'Your Love' and who became a friend after I wrote about his group, and handled their publicity for a time, was also a batchmate in that camp. His contemporary Mike Villegas, whose composition and hit 'Bilanggo' (especially the acoustic version which he impassionedly sung) is a favourite of mine, was also a mentor. The other two camp heads were the prolific Jim Paredes and Vehnee Saturno, both of whom were previous subjects in my articles.

It's an honour that I am a member of FILSCAP, the association of national prominence where you can find the most decorated songwriters in the Philippines. My friend, songwriting coach, and Syato producer—Snaffu Rigor—endorsed me to become a member. The yearly Christmas parties are highlights that allow the ordinary and struggling to line up for a dinner buffet with the multi-awarded and royalty-rich.

One time, Joseph Gonzales and I attended one of these parties and I could feel like we got past our amateurish stage and officially became part of the crème de la crème of Filipino tunesmiths.

However, it soon became apparent that you can't really be recognized unless you have scored a hit or two. There was this game where a member would be called, and he would have to say his piece by singing a hit song he wrote. Dex had a great moment when his name was called and he, of course, had to sing 'Your Love'. There was warm applause in the venue. Obviously, everyone in the room, or the less celebrated if I may say, realized that there was a guy who wrote a classic—the song everybody in my high school loves.

It's always a privilege to be friends with someone who wrote at least one brilliant song. Dex, in one of our chats, revealed that 'Your Love' wasn't even a love song. But a paean to God.

Still, he can't blame the '90s youngsters for thinking it is about romantic love, especially with an opening that addresses someone as the one 'who never lets me sleep'. Two lines later, that same one touches the singer's lips. God must have been pleased. So were the Batang '90s.

Chapter 12

One-Hit Wonder Boy

When I read the name Enrie Cabatino on a Facebook post by FILSCAP that announced his death, I couldn't place it immediately. Call it a middle-age problem, I had been mixing up the people I met in music show business. I sometimes need a trigger or a reminder to refresh my memory.

Looking it up online, I immediately recognized him. He was the one who wrote the song 'Nosi Balasi', one of Pinoy Rock's gems sung effectively by Philippine's Queen of Rock Sampaguita. I like 'Nosi Balasi' largely due to its melancholically rocking melody pushed further by the crazy lead guitar solo. The realization that he had died balled me over.

In 2014, I had met Enrie during a press conference where I met and interviewed Sampaguita for a show she was a part of. He was a quiet, neatly dressed figure, and very approachable. He was definitely involved in the show as a musician. Even if he wasn't, his presence would surely be welcomed by the famous lady rocker who benefited from his gift of song.

Enrie and I were casually conversing that afternoon at a restaurant reserved for the press and rockers. While it was nice to meet and talk to the legendary Sampaguita in person, it was equally thrilling to have met Enrie—another faceless songwriter who contributed a major hit. The public hardly knew him.

95

I asked Enrie how he came up with 'Nosi Balasi' as it was such an interesting title. He said at the time he was writing it, people were trying to jumble words to sound different and hip. The title is a cute jumbling of the expression 'Sino ba sila?' (Who are they?). It is by far one of the best word plays I ever heard.

I included Enrie in my article about the singer who gave his signature composition the street cred. *The Philippine Star* published my writeup titled 'Sampaguita reluctant Pinoy rock goddess'. As I noted in my feature, Enrie penned 'Nosi Balasi' in less than an hour. He also said that Sampaguita 'instantly thought that the song would make it big'.

Enrie had been in my phonebook since that day I met him, until I had to replace my mobile phone unit. Whatever exchange of words we had was deleted.

That he passed away at the tail end of 2020 in a raging Covid-19 pandemic made his death extra heartbreaking. He was so close to surviving the dreaded year that would be remembered for its numerous deaths, from the virus itself and arguably from the air of depression caused by the effects of community quarantine.

I have met people who are in the same league as Enrie—a songwriting talent who wrote one major hit but is relatively unknown. In some instances, they're nearly uncredited when you search about that big song they penned.

But that is life. Songwriters who are not singers or the face of a group behind a hit may find themselves lost in the mix, and their identity not that remarkable. What's exciting about it is the fact that somewhere, someone is singing along to a tune you wrote, and if that person finds you, you'd feel loved and respected. I hoped I made Ernie feel that day I found out he was someone.

Chapter 13

Meds and DJ

There is privilege in being a music beat writer if you are a real musician too. It has allowed me to meet recording artists I used to just listen to. Some of them became my friends: Medwin Marfil, DJ Alvaro, Chad Borja, Richard Reynoso, and Richard Merk to name a few. These are all singers who are household names too. Fortunately, there's something that made them feel comfortable with me the first or second time we interacted. Let me tell you more about the two of them: Meds and DJ.

In June of 2020, while I was busy trying to finish a manuscript for a Beatles fan tribute I hope to publish one day, I texted Meds to ask if he'd like to join a forum for the book. I asked which Beatles song would he choose as his most favourite, that is, if he were allowed to only choose one? He replied after a while: 'Sorry, *kakabasa ko lang neto*. Can I still give you my answer? Text *ko sayo* later.' He added, 'Take care lage, bro. And your family too. Good day!' (Sorry I just read this. Can I still give you my answer? Let me text it to you later. Take care always bro and your family too. Good day!)

Back in high school, my classmates and I went gaga over some of Meds' band True Faith's early hits like 'Perfect', 'Huwag Na Lang Kaya', and 'Muntik Nang Maabot Ang Langit'. I had a

particular liking for 'Sa Puso Ko'. Its composer—a former True
Faith member and co-founder—Kiko Salazar eventually became
a friend as he worked for MCA Music Philippines, a record
company I often visited because of my ties with its Ad Prom
people. One time I told Kiko how I liked his composition, and he
gave me a shy smile about it.

I wonder what the younger version of me would say when he
finds out I am now rubbing elbows with these fellows!

I regularly meet celebrities during press conferences or
privilege interviews. Meds at one point informed me that he took
a line from my review of their album 'Love Parade' to be placed
on a billboard. I saw that one when I was traversing EDSA one
afternoon. It was in one of the buildings near Annapolis Street
in Santolan.

During a presser at the Viva Records office, Meds approached
me to say hello. He mentioned he liked a post about my wedding
anniversary and that if and when I want him to sing for a special
family occasion, he would. That gave me an idea to do a renewal
of vows with my wifey when the right time comes.

The beloved front man who married his San Francisco-based
true love named Mark Angeles had a voice that was especially
notable for the fact that RJ of Syato had some vocal resemblance
to his timbre. We were pegged as a True Faith–like band when we
were tapped to be signed by Ivory.

Naturally, our self-titled album sounded like a band highly
influenced by True Faith. It added more weight when later
I became friends with this small-boned guy with a big, enthralling
voice. I always love hearing his oohs and aahs, with his mouth
looking like that of Peter Cetera singing. Meds' a true embodiment
of small standing tall.

DJ, on the other hand, sealed her spot in the Philippine music
scene with one song, in the same way that Sinead O'Connor
would be remembered by one song—'Nothing Compares 2 U'.

DJ wrote her classic 'Ang Tipo Kong Lalaki' (My Kind of Guy), a brave piece ahead of its time. She reminded me that we met at FILSCAP as members, and then I wrote about her.

I even recommended a bass player to play for her sets. I couldn't take her up on her offer because I can't play bass for a band doing three sets a night, and mostly covers. I wasn't born to focus on covering songs. My heart says I should do originals. I want to nurture my passion to create.

My bands do cover songs only because of the need to, and mostly tracks I really like hearing. They're not that many. Some of the cover songs I did with Syato were also performed by my much-later band The Pub Forties, notably R.E.M's 'One I Love' and The Cure's 'Lovesong'.

I was a bit surprised and felt happy when DJ finally found the man who was the love of her life. Before this, I would see her on TV being linked to starlet Aleck Bovick.

At FILSCAP gatherings, she's among the beloved women and you can tell some people find her sexy. '*Maginoo pero medyo bastos*' (Gentleman but a bit naughty) is really a brilliant line to have in a song. When she sang it, it sounded like she opened a door to women's sexuality back in the good ol' '90s. Countless pakipots (shy-types) may have smiled hearing the line while touchy boys might have felt their egos boosted.

I wrote a song called 'Babae Blues' and initially I had her in mind to sing it. Then I could hear Cooky Chua of Color It Red— another '90s hit band—sing it. It should help that I know her too. I'm not in a hurry when it comes to collaborating with a celebrity singer. That opportunity can wait.

I was able to collaborate with DJ Alvaro when The Pub Forties appeared on her online show, which we shot at the place of our guitarist Vince Borromeo in Scout Alcaraz in Quezon City. The room is actually a law office, run by Vince's family and he and his wife, Reggie, have always been gracious hosts.

I felt goosebumps when she praised my band, and commented on a song I wrote. She gave her thumbs up to 'Road Rage', the first original song The Pub Forties recorded, which I penned after the deactivation of Syato. I heard her trying to provide harmonies as we played it for everyone watching on Facebook live. It was a proud moment for me. Here's a one-hit wonder woman who gained industry respect jamming with my band and valuing me as her friend.

Chapter 14

Ultraelectroatomic Bands

My work as a music writer got me to interview and write about the two most significant bands that sprouted from the '90s Philippine rock alternative scene—Eraserheads and Rivermaya. They're also the two bestselling Filipino groups.

At the time that I'm writing this, both acts have a combined five albums among the fifty biggest sellers in local music history. Rivermaya had their first three albums on the list, while the pioneering Eraserheads owned the top-selling band-crafted album in *Cutterpillow*. Their other big seller, *Circus*, was the band's sophomore effort. Their greatest hits anthology was also cited in the list.

In 2001, I was fairly new at *Manila Bulletin* when I was assigned to write about Christmas tunes. A few years ago, Eraserheads came up with a Christmas album called *Fruitcake*. On that note I was able to find a way to get in touch with their handler. The arrangement was for me to interview Ely Buendia, the band's songwriter and essentially the man behind every Eraserheads hit, prior to their show at a bar in Quiapo, Manila.

That November evening, I brought my brother, Rockefeller, along. He's an Eraserheads super fan, and I pulled him in so he could meet his idol in person. It felt good that my work had allowed my brother to meet Ely. I, too, was an Ely fan but, of course, The Beatles were my main heroes.

The goal was to interview Ely and quote him in the article that I was going to write for a special supplement fold related to Christmas. We were poised to watch the band's show too.

Ely was relatively nice that night and he even accommodated me and my brother for our photo-op request. He was the last member to arrive at the venue, which gave us a chance to talk to the other three as we waited for him.

Incidentally, the interview was set on the same day George Harrison died. Bassist Buddy Zabala reminded me of that during our small talk. My brother had his old Eraserheads tapes signed by the four of them. All were dressed in their usual casual clothes—shirts, jeans, and rubber shoes, which they turned into some rock fashion trend since they became famous in the early '90s. Save for Ely, none of them had the aura of a rock star.

Drummer Raymund Marasigan even invited us to hang out with them after their show. We politely declined because we were kind of not prepared. I didn't have much money as I was a newbie in the biz, and admittedly, I hadn't practised socializing much, let alone with so-called rock royalties.

Three months after that encounter with Ely and the boys, I would read in the showbiz column 'Scuttlebutt' that Ely had left Eraserheads. It was stated that, somehow, punctuality, among others, were reasons behind the clashes within the band.

The evening that we saw them, we didn't see Ely huddled with the others. Looking back, my brother and I saw a band about to crumble. That made the encounter poignantly special. Their live performance was great. It would take a few years before I'd see them again together on stage in a couple of reunion shows.

Kaye was pregnant when we watched them reunited in 2008, at an open grounds concert cut short at mid-set after Ely was rushed to hospital due to chest pains. By that time, they were already a nostalgia act.

As for Rivermaya, there was no chance for me to interview their classic line-up since Bamboo, the lead singer, had already left the group by 1998. I was still in college then.

I had warmer encounters with the Rivermaya members. I exchanged text messages with chief songwriter Rico Blanco when he was already the front man. At one press conference, after he went solo, he mentioned my name and told everyone that I had been covering his career for quite some time.

I once told him that 'Shattered Like' is a Rivermaya track I love. I guess I would have gotten less respect if I had said '214', which is everybody's favourite. Sometime later I received a CD gift of their greatest hits from him, with his message and signature.

When I finally interviewed Rivermaya in person in 2013, the mild-mannered drummer Mark Escueta was already the leader and sole original member on board. Bass player Nathan Azarcon had left the group in 2001 and formed a band with Bamboo two years later. They went on to score some hits of their own.

I remember Bamboo telling me that he's unable to see himself performing with the name Rivermaya written behind him. That's quite a pity considering the superb vocal character that he gave to the band's most successful albums. However, a consolation is that he finally rejoined the group for a much-awaited reunion concert in early 2024.

In the few times I got to chat with members of both bands, I saw their differing personalities. Ely, in his post-Eraserheads years, seemed to have developed a deadpan humour, which to some extent is cool. When I interviewed his post-Eraserheads band, Pupil, he described some of his songs as 'brain farts'. He couldn't say the name Erasherheads, so instead he remarked, 'that band was derivative'. I found that quite ironic because he wrote the bulk of their discography. I thought he still needed time to make peace with his past self. I notice it's common for big-name artists to want to get away from the suffocation of fame. It's human nature to feel lonely at the top.

Well, if having a great songwriting skill gives one the right to act in a certain way, then Ely has all day to be him. What a blessing that we mortal souls get to hear the sound of his brain farting!

The songwriting specialist of Rivermaya, Rico Blanco has always tried to connect, especially if he knows that a fan or a critic is for real. After a gig during his active solo years, he stood up when I approached him for a small chat. I suggested that the Rivermaya story, for all its juicy, intersecting plots, ought to be told by way of a book—not that I want him to tap me to write it.

Bamboo, a front man for the ages in the annals of Pinoy Rock, does his best to be kind to music journalists and I am a happy recipient. At a press conference while he was being interviewed by a TV crew, he saw me seated at a corner and he nodded to say hello. When I was given a few minutes to chat with him, he shook my hands and made me feel I was talking to a close friend. Maybe it was because of my distinct look, with curly hair and fedora hat, that made it easier for me to connect with artists. Ryde has a picture with him as a toddler.

Mark, who found true love with famous Filipina actress Jolina Magdangal, is like that friend of yours in college who never changes in spite of fame. Calling someone 'bro' is second nature to him. At a gig where I was covering his group, he introduced me to Jolina whose breakout hit as a singer, 'Laging Tapat', was the song Syato did a rock cover of for a compilation of great radio hits.

Eraserheads and Rivermaya meant a lot to many music fans. They were forerunners of our youth; I was a teenager during the '90s and they spoke directly to my generation. The latter have a track called 'Awit Ng Kabataan' (Song of the Youth), the former have 'Para Sa Masa' (For the Masses). That I was privileged to dissect their music and interact with them in a professional manner mattered to me both as a music journalist and musician. I felt it was necessary to meet them so I could somehow demystify the myth. It made it easy for me to navigate the reality of the music scene and the world of artists in general knowing that gods are real men.

*With wife Kaye Villagomez-Losorata, the inspiration for some of
Yugel's compositions, including 'Stop The World', 'Sayo Lang',
'Sticking By', 'Sandalan', and 'Hosanna Kapiling Ka'*

Chapter 15

Jay Walking

The original members of four officemates from a newspaper company actually had a fifth member who was not an employee of *Manila Bulletin*—Jay Flores. Yes, he was the same Jay that Chris and I formed The Dreamers with. One afternoon I arrived home from work and found Jay playing computer games with one of my brothers. He came by unannounced and totally out of nowhere. It may have been a few years since I last saw him. That's very Jay. He'd surprise you with a grin, as if saying, 'Here, bro, I'm back in your life. Give me a hug.'

That hug came with an offer from me for him to join Syato because our lead guitarist at the time, JP Santiago, was going abroad. He accepted it without skipping a beat. It was not a bad choice for a last-minute addition before the day we were set to sign the recording contract.

Many of our gigs were attended by family members of Jay. They would come in hordes to support and cheer for us. His father, who wants to be called Ka Roger, has a printing business and Jay initiated the production of Syato posters, lyric booklets for the songs in our album, and other merchandise to promote our band. He was a happy lad now that he had become a recording artist because he decided to reconnect with me!

Just like that, Jay, the boy who was the ringleader in the early stage of The Dreamers, was again my bandmate. We had a few, odd discussions about whether or not to inform Chris of this development. But I was too busy trying to fulfil a dream and Chris was out of my life anyway. We were disconnected for quite some time and I couldn't be bothered. It was a mistake on my part not to reach out to Chris and initiate some form of reconciliation.

In the back of my head, I knew I wouldn't be able to reject Chris if and when he expressed the desire to jump in. Truth be told, Jay was just at the right place at the right time and anyway, Chris wouldn't fit in a band with RJ and Joseph taking care of the vocals and rhythm guitar, respectively. I felt there would be clashes because of their personalities.

Jay fitted naturally into Syato. Years out of college and seeing it as his salvation, he knew where he stood. He acknowledged that what we needed was a subordinate, not another leader. Although not consciously planned, he took the role of the odd guy who would say quirky things during interviews and appear on stage like he's just happy to be part of the ride. Out of the blue he told everyone that he was adopting the stage name 'Nelo'. I never heard anyone call him by that time.

During a provincial gig, he went on stage and revealed that his guitar gadget had no batteries. A friend of the band who was with us had to buy new batteries in a rush.

While Jay was enjoying his position as the last guy to make the cut, I would see RJ and Joseph puzzled about what to make of him. That actually was Jay's advantage, he was way different from any of us. The four of us who were officemates had the tendency to sound too corporate and were consciously trying to do things in the most righteous manner. Jay couldn't care. He didn't have a boss as he was practically jobless. He didn't have an image to protect as he was playing the role of a bohemian to a T. He got in and made us look at how he saw the world—with amusement.

RJ and Joseph, though they never outwardly said it, knew that they were being perceived as the band front men. It was a consolation that I got to sing harmonies with them. When they sang together, it was proof enough that Syato could sing.

Joseph's songwriting locked in with how we should sound as a band; eyed as a rebirth of Manila Sound, not a direct copy but having its essentials like vocal harmonies, relatable poetry, and steady playing—just feeling the groove and not being flamboyant. Joseph's composition 'Paano Ba' was for me his best work, in spite of the fact that 'Lubusan' and 'Kailanman' were given more attention in the narrative. This proved right when this song was picked by the late blockbuster director Wenn Deramas as a sub-theme for a movie he directed starring comedienne Ai Ai delas Alas and action star-politician Bong Revilla. I felt privileged being the other half of the Joseph-Yugel songwriting tandem.

Having a day job meant we were too tired to get regular gigs at night. We didn't have much in our repertoire. One time, the late great balladeer Rico J. Puno, whom I interviewed and wrote about, asked us to play in his bar in Makati City. We did it one night in what was a rush decision to experience something extraordinary. We played in front of a few bar patrons that got in early that Saturday and Rico J. himself, who happened to have tagged another famous recording artist in Hajji Alejandro.

We thought a few songs would do. But we were asked to play more. You wouldn't believe but we had to do our song 'Sa Ulan' twice, out of impulse. We hadn't rehearsed and we only had about seven songs we were confident enough to play that evening!

*Starting off as a rhythm guitarist before moving to bass guitar,
Yugel also plays the piano/keyboard. (Photo by Ariel Obera)*

Chapter 16

Let's Play Syato Forever

The five-year run of Syato, from its beginnings in early 2002, was a special period that also covered much of my time as writer-employee of *Manila Bulletin*. The experience necessarily boosted my morale both as a musician and writer.

Without that stretch in my life, I may have gone on to another field and abandoned writing and music altogether.

Once Syato was launched as a signee of Ivory Records, whose classic roster of artists included successful groups such as Side A, Wolfgang, The Company, and our contemporary MYMP, a string of meaty gigs came filling up our schedule. I remember we appeared on MYX Live—a famous TV spot for mainstream acts—and there was a couch interview with the celebrity lady host Iya Villania.

We did on-air performances on the radio. I became friends with the likes of household DJs like Tito Potato and T-Bowne because of these FM station tours. My wife Kaye even used her connections in the entertainment industry to book us TV performances and other cool gigs. We appeared on the lifestyle channel of ABS-CBN, thrilled to have been seen and heard on mainstream TV.

One time, we went up to Baguio, the summer capital of the Philippines because of its cold weather, to front for the hit band

Parokya Ni Edgar. I am a fan of the group and so it was surreal performing on a show they were headlining. Years later, I became friends with their bassist Buwi Meneses after I wrote in the paper about the supergroup he became a part of.

There were a series of shopping mall shows we did where we would be ushered like stars at the backstage of an elevated platform wherein the drums and amplifiers had been set up. These gigs put you closer to everyday people. In the Philippines, to see faces from all walks of life, you go to the malls. It is a country whose urban people find it almost a necessity to get inside a mall to take a break from the heat of the sun and be freshened by centralized air conditioning.

In one of our mall gigs, I saw in the crowd a bloke I didn't expect to be there—Omay Gorecho. Clothed like a hippie with a fondness for beads, Omay was one of the photographers I had featured on the 'Picture Perfect' fold of *Manila Bulletin* in which I was a regular profiler of interesting lensmen and women. After the performance he approached and said he came with his girlfriend to support us. That kind of gesture melts the heart, and I experienced such a show of appreciation numerous times when performing with Syato, even with the succeeding line-up that followed.

In November of 2005, we played in the highly regarded Hard Rock Café in Makati. The bar could be found within the Glorietta-Greenbelt mall complex. You bet we were more prepared as we did a forty-five-minute set and our performance earned a good review from one of the music writers who watched us live.

A year later, we were commissioned to play at a homecoming event among batchmates. We did a number of covers, including Frankie Valli's 'Can't Take My Eyes Off You'. The crowd was there to dance to classic numbers. We did good as the person who contacted us informed us. I'm amazed at how we pulled that off. We were not used to playing à la showband, and we were out on the road mainly to promote a full-length album of originals. We happily posed for a group shot in the middle of the stage after we were done with our set.

None of us realized that was the last time we would be playing music together. Somehow it felt we had come a long way from our first gig years back during a Christmas party of *Manila Bulletin* employees. What happened in between may be a small thing for a big-name act. But for us, it was a journey of a lifetime.

Many Filipinos desire to go abroad for greener pastures. So, we weren't surprised that Mike decided to move to another country. He never said that our band couldn't go on further. It was a personal decision for him to fly to New Zealand where he is still residing to this day.

At the same time, Joseph had decided to focus on his family. When one time I dropped by the *Manila Bulletin* office as I already shifted professionally to a freelance journalist, he noted, 'I'm giving up something good for something better.'

I couldn't argue with his decision. He wanted to settle for good. I wouldn't dare tell him I've been married even before we entered the recording studio to properly record our songs. Well, what works for me may not work for others.

I knew that when Joseph left, I won't be able to convince RJ to continue steering the wheel with me. That's the dynamic of Joseph and RJ's relationship. It was a partnership. One joined the band because the other did. And I didn't feel jealous over their closeness. In fact, I'm grateful that they allowed their friendship to be part of Syato's fibre.

Jay was always being Jay. He was back in my life one day, and when he felt our run was over, off he went without a shudder. We closed this chapter of Syato in 2006.

There was not a moment I sat and cried about that point in Syato's run. Unlike when The Dreamers broke up, Syato had quite an experience, especially in its final two years as a record label signed act. We had been part of the mainstream music scene for a while, and we had an album of our originals.

As a writer I had been gaining ground meeting important people, writing about them, and in some instances, playing music for them. I was part of the music community both as a writer and a musician. I have stacks of unrecorded songs in my vault. Nothing was stopping me from continuing.

Chorus: Syato Reset

Chapter 1

Blessed to Believe

It may have been advisable to just think of a new band name and kickstart a new chapter in my life as a musician. But something within led me to keep going under the name Syato. I felt Syato needed continuity, even if it meant having to do it with new faces and significantly different sound.

While initially I had doubts over the name Syato, I soon came to love it, thanks to the little victories we had experienced since carrying the name. Back at the ASAP TV launch, one of the celebrity hosts who interviewed us after our performance saw us backstage preparing to leave the dressing room. He shouted, 'Syato!'

I couldn't think of a better name, I guess. But frankly speaking, it really felt like I wasn't in a position to shut the door that Syato had opened. For me, it was a disservice to our efforts as officemates coming together and becoming recording artists to the apparent shock of those who may have been mocking us for our guts.

So, one day in 2007 I asked for RJ and Joseph's blessing for me to prolong using our band's name as I look for new bandmates. They gave me a sweet smile. It was around this time that I heard Mike tell me that I had been the de facto leader all the while. For that alone—for contributing my energy to the cause more than any of us—he said I deserved to carry on the name.

It was a little personal triumph getting the blessing of your newly ex bandmates. An odd jam happened right after as I asked former Dreamer members Mike and Val to come over and play with me. Perhaps it had to do with how Syato turned out that they immediately agreed. They didn't ask why Chris was not around.

Sadly, around that time Chris and I were still in the middle of a fallout after he found out that a former Chris-Yugel song, 'Elkyu', had landed on the Syato album and he was not mentioned as a composer. This happened because I was told we couldn't have a third songwriter credited in the album apart from Joseph Gonzales and me, thus, I took out 'Elkyu's' bridge part, which had Chris' melody and lyrics. I loved the song and thought it had to be on the album even if I had to drop Chris' portion. It was a selfish move and I later apologized.

Anyway, around that period, I was already becoming buddies with my brother-in-law, Mark Villagomez, who was part of a heavy rock band himself. He has that manly build and a kind-looking handsomeness complemented by his shaved head that allows his sharp facial features to glow. More importantly, he sounds truly handsome when he sings. I really could not and would rather not explain that. But there are singing voices that sound like the guy behind it is not good-looking at all.

I had been married to Mark's sister for two years. They were especially close as they didn't have other siblings. I cannot recall the day Kaye recommended her brother as a good candidate for my band's lead singer slot. I had heard Mark sing karaoke during family gatherings and felt he wasn't a bad choice.

Out of thin air, I asked him if he'd like to sing a song I wrote. He excitedly said yes.

Inside a rehearsal studio built beside a gym, three past members of The Dreamers jammed with a potential new Syato vocalist. Mark sang one of my compositions, 'Drive On', a track that only got recorded much later and with another band. But that day the song gave Mark a role he'd embrace for the next several years. He was officially my bandmate after that jam.

I also realized that the tension between me and Chris would escalate further if Syato continued with Mike and Val on board. Somehow there wasn't much chemistry among the three of us without Chris, and I made the decision to restart with a clean state. No former bandmates for the new-look Syato to be fronted by Mark.

My thankful brother-in-law began finding ways to help reform Syato. I think his wishes manifested when he located a pure guitarist named Erickson Villarmino playing under a tree not far from the compound where we were residing. I was with my in-laws for a couple of years as we were waiting for the completion of a condo unit that Kaye and I planned to move into.

On meeting Erickson, nicknamed Meng, Mark must have felt the same way I did back in the university the day I met Chris and Jay. He sang another composition to Meng, one I had penned and introduced to Mark, called 'Broken Tuesday'. The thinly framed boy who was still in his late teens showed off by coming up with an impromptu guitar ad lib for the song. Mark asked him to join the band right away.

Meng happened to have seen a couple of music magazines that featured Syato and thought he had landed the gig of a lifetime. He went to tell the news to his own pal named JM Delos Santos.

He later told us that JM couldn't believe that he was recruited to be a member of Syato.

We needed a drummer, so Meng pulled in JM to play drums. JM could play drums, but it wasn't his instrument. Yet, we considered him the fact that he had the physical assets, one that could make girls take a second look—not that I knew how to determine if a boy is attractive or not. Kaye helped me decide on that.

With my little marketing experience as a newbie in the news asking companies to place broadsheet ads, and my growing knowledge for publicity work that I had started doing in a freelance capacity, I sensed that having JM in the band would help us get the attention of the adoring female crowd. I wasn't wrong.

JM had a dynamic, nice guy aura. It felt okay letting him join. In no time he became the group's girl magnet. Someone had to replace him on drums but that was fine because he was better off wooing girls in the crowd from the front.

I could say I had a hand in the development of both Meng and JM as musical artists. They continued being musicians even after their Syato days.

I assessed Meng to be a superb guitarist, with his already deep know-how in playing blues and jazz, or his ability to understand things like the pentatonic scale. Though musically gifted, he played with borrowed guitars and was unkempt most of the time. He was a bohemian digging through his inner self.

Meng didn't even have money to go to the dentist for a much-needed fix. I had to finance that myself. He deserved the help. He was evidently a prodigy, and an asset to the band. His guitar licks all over the album proved that note after note, weep after weep.

He was a welcome addition to the band, and I allowed him to bring in his cousin Macky Brosas to replace JM on drums. My idea was to put JM in the front with Mark, playing rhythm guitar. The combination proved effective. The new Syato basically had a couple of visually appealing front men and a pure guitar player who could take the solo spotlight with ease and bravura at any given moment.

Macky was just there to keep the beat steady, and I knew where I stood, being the band leader playing the bass guitar, writing the songs, and breathing soul in the band day in and out.

Chapter 2

Smorgasbord

The big difference between Syato's first and second albums, both of which came out in CDs and then later in digital formats, was how the two sets of band personnel chose and treated the songs on them.

The first, the self-titled debut album, was more defined—pop songs, romantic Tagalog, with vocal harmonies, and a touch of mild rock.

The second, called *Sticking By*—which was a little personal statement about how I had stayed in the band regardless of its future's uncertainties—was a smorgasbord, with various genres and subjects all pulled into one place. Me and my young, motley crew of untried musicians tried to prove something without a record label backing us up.

With our record contract expired, we took the route of an independent artist. I had absolute control over new songs to record so I ended up being the writer for all ten songs on *Sticking By*.

JM, who would eventually write a couple of tracks for Syato, had yet to learn how to write tunes. I take pride in having seen him become a songwriter in his own right. He sure learned a thing or two from me.

With most bands churning out originals usually dominated by one or two composers among its members, I found it amusing to have a whole album composed of songs written solely by me. I enjoyed having such control, but I acknowledge that being part of a collaboration is definitely more fun.

Despite not having a label, I thought we delivered a decent album of ten songs, just like its self-titled predecessor issued three years back. In an article written by Bong Godinez of *PEP.ph* and uploaded on July 28, 2009, months after the release of the album, he said, 'All of the songs included in the record offer interesting stories intertwined with catchy melodic tunes.'

In the first Syato album, I had to play by ear how my songs would be accommodated, and which among my collaborations with Joseph Gonzales deserved to make the cut. It was a bit of a concern on my part that Joseph and RJ were more of a match musically. I was an outsider, and I thought my compositions would only serve as fillers. RJ's voice appeared to fit Joseph's kind of writing.

While the first album was crafted in a recording studio with a rich history, *Sticking By* had to be done at a virtually unknown venue named Aeon Studio in Manila. I met the studio manager Joy Balubayan when I featured in the newspaper a band he handled. He offered the studio for the recording of our album for a measly sum.

We recorded the whole album for weeks, with lots of overnight sessions that included some drinking. I was really having a good time doing it all again, this time with a younger pool of musicians. The new Syato, ragtag as we were, with none of the new members having a deep background in performing and recording, was a hungrier team and wanted to have more fun while recording.

The original members of Syato didn't have these brandy and beer sessions. Our camaraderie was carved through the regular working hours that we were obliged to spend in the same office.

The new Syato were a bunch of spitfire men looking for a big break.

By my observation, Joseph had a clear choice of what kind of songs he'd write. I was adapting to the identity of our band. When I noticed that alternative rock was the common ground of Syato's new personnel, I knew the compositions to be recorded should veer away from pop and get in the area of rock. Mark specialized in growling, and he had that rock star stance. The first Syato comprised of old souls while the new Syato had a good dose of youth.

Since I was the leader and the second Syato's only composer at that time, I had the luxury of picking which songs from my songwriting vault would have to be recorded.

So, there we were at Aeon Studio in late 2007 and early 2008, recording our parts for a ten-song album. There was one night when Mark recorded his vocals for almost half of the content. Either he was in his element, or we were pressed for time. Listening to the album now, I still would argue that Mark's vocals were right for many of the songs, especially 'Bighani' (Amazed), 'Kung Wala Ka Na' (If You're Gone) and 'Gabing Bilog Ang Buwan' (Full Moon Night). The way he sung the words sounded authentic to me, like when he sang *Di ko alam ang binabalak mo / Marahil ay ito na ang dulo*' (Not sure what do you intend to do / Perhaps this is the end) to open 'Kung Wala Ka Na'. Listening to him made me forget that I had written those words and the melody myself. Something in his voice told me that the song was personal to him.

My young team accepted their roles well. I remember Meng and JM spending time working out the riff and guitar arrangement for 'Gabing Bilog Ang Buwan' (Full Moon Night). That gave the song its hard rock direction. Back in college when I wrote it, I imagined a folksy ode to the inner mental workings of a philosophical mind. It has its twist, that the thinker is plain and simple lunatic, hence, the obsession for the striking beauty or haunting splendour of the full moon.

The track order, which I did by alternating English and Tagalog tracks, put the rock-out song side by side with a new wave-styled tune I also started composing back in UST—'Broken Tuesday'. As far as my songwriting is concerned, this eightyish piece is a highlight, containing what to me is my strongest verse tune.

Interestingly, my wife, Kaye, noticed that my original chorus to this song sounded unfit to the verses. She suggested that the chorus must continue the mood of the verses. If I recall it correctly, the first bar of the melody line of the eventual chorus was something she hummed to stress her point. I liked it and I worked my way from there.

I played the keyboard riff and adlib on 'Broken Tuesday'. The instrumental notes that I played impromptu while demoing the track ended up on the record. Original Syato drummer Mike Santos was witness to that. Songwriting embraces pretty accidents. You just have to make sure you've pressed the recording button.

In the album title song, I even asked Mark to growl a full verse. It's an empowering song about holding on to someone who matters to you, especially in troubling times. It's a shoutout to sticking to whatever is the plan.

I would have chosen that song to be the album's closer. But a track called 'Heroes' took the slot by virtue of it being the loudest of all the ten tracks. It featured Mark's longest growl on record.

As we usually end our bar gigs with 'Heroes' as that vocal-shredding encore, let me say that the song's best part is the restrained refrain, saying, 'Fight until you die / For there is life for those behind / Forever.'

Attuned to the album's quite bizarre track ordering, 'Heroes' was preceded by 'Panaginip Lamang', a pop-tinged alternative rock I wrote way back in the '90s for my then-ultimate crush. It may have been my most radio-friendly contribution to The Dreamers. There's a slight difference as to how Syato's version came to be.

I made the mistake of not doing everything to get Chris credited in 'Elkyu' from the first album so this time around I made sure we will be credited together.

We tried 'Panaginip Lamang' to become the follow up to lead-single 'Tibo'. Sadly, our friend, Espie Eusebio, who put the latter in the Love Radio playlist rotation, was no longer in the thick of things or may have already lost interest in us by the time it was to be released. The song still made it as the theme song on the final episode of a Kim Chiu—starred series called 'Your Song'. Thanks to the efforts of Evelyn Seale, another label executive who has become a dear friend like Espie.

In 2020 Chiu became a novelty singer with a viral hit while I was still, as you may expect, looking for my first major hit. Actresses or actors become hitmakers in the Philippines!

For all my years of making music and recording compositions, I have learned to appreciate the fact that having a hit song is not the lone barometer of success. Being able to write a song, record, and release it is not the easiest thing to do. That alone is an accomplishment. Can't do nothing about some people putting so much value to face over talent.

I believe that had some of my songs been sung by famous faces, they would have become hits by now.

Playing the acoustic guitar with which the author wrote a number of his compositions, including the radio hit 'Tibo' and some records that made the Spotify's New Music Friday playlist, namely, 'Drive On', 'Pagsapit Ng Unos', and 'Next Big Thing'

Chapter 3

Concert Scene

With my profession as a music writer whose byline appears on national broadsheets and online news sites, I've been privileged to be present at several Manila concerts featuring popular acts without having to buy tickets.

Either I would be given production passes or complimentary tickets.

Some of my favourite bands that I have seen performing their biggest hits live include Duran Duran, Spandau Ballet, Tears for Fears, America, Gin Blossoms, Fra Lippo Lippi, OMD, Pet Shop Boys, and some more. A number of them I got to see twice. I saw Maroon 5 live in Manila at least three times, each show as exciting as the previous one. The group led by the charismatically high-pitched Adam Levine managed to churn out new hits before embarking on another world tour, so they always had something fresh to offer.

I was happily present when Linkin Park performed at the Mall of Asia Arena in Pasay, Metro Manila. It was one of the most electrifying modern rock shows I have witnessed, especially with me knowing many of their numbers by heart considering I highly fancied the band's music, particularly their groundbreaking, scene-changing debut album *Hybrid Theory*. Personally, it's the best rock album I've heard in the twenty-first century. Its template of short, melodic rock tunes is classic, anchored on the high-octane lead vocals of the late Chester Bennington and the confident, testosterone-fused rapping of Mike Shinoda. I felt that the show featured a group with its frontman giving it all out. Chester's growls and screams really struck to a new millennium battling its frustrations. Linkin Park's music is accessible because its melodies and lyrics are not hard to chew. It's just the kind of gum a hard-working basketball player needs on the court.

Having seen that show made Bennington's suicide in 2017 difficult to comprehend. We thought he had already exorcised his demons through their world-admired songs. That wasn't enough for him. His skill and showmanship fit the new millennium crowd, along with the dazzling concert lights and booming surround sound. Everyone should just be thankful that he happened to pass by and chose to stay as long as he could. Thank you, Chester.

It's ironic that by the time I'm seeing big concerts for free, pampered as I usually attend press conferences scheduled before the shows, many of the artists at hand are no longer the ones I would do anything just to hear. Curiously, Linkin Park and Incubus are the last of what I perceived as bands whose music I could really dig. I have seen Incubus multiple times, and I couldn't get enough of them. Their music is like a bridge of the '90s and the 2000s. Those bands that came after Linkin Park and Incubus are mostly acts I found lacking in artistry or allure, which I believe bands I heard in my youth possessed.

Sorry to the fans of Fall Out Boy. I think they're a sellout for making the bass player answer media questions, and in effect serves as the face of the band even if he's not the main singer and composer. The lead singer appears odd, somewhat showing a low-profile-but-in-control attitude. I don't buy their gimmick and their melodies don't hit me right. Perhaps it's the generation-gap thing. I was adjusting to my sudden incapacity to dig new music as

I gave up on listening to the band's work after they released a song with a music video where they're trying to be goofy.

My writing about music is strongly influenced by my preferences as a music fan. I cannot fool readers by saying something is passable when I think it does not work for me. I am objective as necessary, but reviewing music is subjective. I wouldn't right away say I like a supergroup. I don't care much about who's on board. I need their music to speak to me.

I am an old soul so naturally classic bands or those influenced by the sound of the past have an advantage. So, when there's a classic artist landing in Manila to perform, you can expect I will try my best to get a seat at the show. A number of them I got to see more than once—a reflection of how I have kept myself writing for the music scene beat. I was there when people booed political couple Mar Roxas and Korina Sanchez after they were shown on the screen at a Tears for Fears concert. It was the eve of the presidential election and Roxas was bound to lose.

I was there, too, when Toto was also frowned at because they played only snippets of their biggest hits in a medley form. The ploy looked as if they were playing the crowd that was patiently waiting for them to perform their most popular songs. Not even the flamboyance of Steve Lukather's playing could save the day. He must have forgotten that the crowd was not entirely composed of technically gifted guitarists, or those pretending they understand music better than most people but can't write a tune or play a good solo themselves.

My concert-watching life also fell under the period where a lot of lady acts dominated the charts. I've covered concerts featuring the likes of Britney Spears, Katy Perry, Beyoncé, and Christina Aguilera. I recall Christina didn't sing her debut hit 'Genie In A Bottle' during her show and I felt bad about it. Perhaps she was tired of performing the track. I was in college when that song became a hit so obviously, it's a song I wanted to hear her sing live.

Some classic acts I've seen perform proved why they're legendary. In 2011, I closed my eyes while Don McLean sang his acoustic hits, his voice hanging on every note and filling up a packed, but quiet Araneta Coliseum or Big Dome as it is dubbed by the media, intently listening to every lyric and melody line he delivered. His voice is ageless. He must have been in his sixties singing 'Vincent' and 'And I Love You So' like he's in the 1970s when he burst into the music scene. It's a pity to find out that he allegedly mistreated his wife of twenty-seven years. Some talents are best living their lives on stage!

I also got to see The Cascades live. Yes, they're alive. My good friend Danee Samonte who's known for bringing to Manila select acts from the '60s made sure that they appear in flesh and once and for all throw off the myth that the group died from a plane crash. They were just named like a plane carrying them was destined to hit the ground. Buddy Holly, Ritchie Valens, and The Big Bopper were the ones whose plane actually cascaded on an early February flight, that day the music died in 1959. The Don knows that for sure.

Chapter 4

Marriage and Family

In the early part of 2000, amid a new century and millennium I had begun my run in the print media industry, and then I also met my soulmate.

Katherine Ann Villagomez was writing for the special lifestyle page *C'est La Vie* when I found her seated at her desk in a corner near the Xerox copy machine in our department. She was a buxom young lady who talked no nonsense. I was immediately smitten. The first time I saw her recognizing me, I trembled and almost tripped in front of her. She laughed. We fell in love.

I quickly observed that Kaye had a very good sense of humour wrapped in wit. She later said that when our common friend first introduced me to her, she was actually hoping that I was not the guy who wanted to know her name. When I would eat my words when talking—in other words when I'd stammer—she'd ask if I needed a glass of water. I would describe her as 'the girl who makes me laugh'.

Apart from being my girlfriend and best friend, Kaye also pushed me to get deep into my writing potential. She would remind me to read more and consistently watch movies, documentaries, and TV series that were worth binging. I was flattered when she heard 'Panaginip Lamang' and gave me a sweet smile, obviously to let me know that she found my songwriting skill commendable.

In 2004, I asked Kaye to come with me to attend mass at UST church. It was a return to our alma mater. Kaye, a journalism graduate, was my junior in the college of Arts and Letters. We never met there but I think I may have seen her once or twice in the building. We were destined to meet in a newspaper company. She believes in destiny and in facing uncertainties with a leap of faith.

Inside the church of the oldest university in the Philippines, I proposed with an engagement ring. *'Let's take a leap of faith!'*

I knew I married the love of my life when on our trip to Bangkok, Thailand, right after our wedding, she expressed how worried she was when she thought I got lost on my train ride to meet her after a movie premiere she'd attended. I only failed to alight on the right station, hence, I got delayed. I hadn't lost my way, what I'd actually lost was our wedding ring, which I'd forgotten in the restroom of our hotel room. We thought it was a bad omen for our marriage. But we're still together nearly two decades since we tied the knot in 2005, the year the first album of Syato was released. What a year that was, and I've been wearing a replica of our actual wedding ring since then.

Our union was blessed with a beautiful boy in 2009, the year Syato enjoyed radio airplay. Kaye named him Rhythm Jude, inspired by The Beatles classic 'Hey Jude', which she shortened to Ryde. Turned out that Ryde, a place in the Isle of Wight, had to do with The Beatles' 'Ticket to Ride'. So, in the age of Facebook and Instagram, Ticket to Ryde is our boy's hashtag.

Kaye and I are both basketball fans, both of the Philippines' PBA and US's NBA. That may have rubbed off to Ryde. He was shooting balls before he could talk. From his toddler years we would play one on one. When he reached his teenage years, he could already beat me at almost every scrimmage. My wife, in particular, has been Ryde's regular companion in his basketball activities, like in attending the Cholo Camp training program, joining the Batang PBA, and playing for the flag in Guam.

Kaye and Ryde have always been my rock. They serve as inspiration for the songs I write. When I'm feeling down, I just think that I have them both as my last line of defence. I can't imagine going through life, with all the challenges I face being a writer and a musician, without them.

I remember one evening, sometime before the pandemic, we were stuck in traffic after one of Ryde's Saturday sessions in Makati for Cholo Camp. I remember our kid thanking us for cheering for him during the just-concluded game, where he had performed so well, he'd led his team to victory. His mom was driving—as I could not drive—and I was seated at the back, as I always do when it's the three of us. He motioned to me, seated in the passenger seat, 'It's traffic, Daddy. We're family.'

There was no need for him to explain what he meant. I just asked him for a high five.

Chapter 5

Pole Dancing Queen

At a press conference, I encountered a starlet who had graced the big screen when I was still in teens. I found out she had become a professional pole dancer. Her name's Belinda Bright and I always thought that was just a screen name. The way she seriously talked about her affair with the pole changed the way I viewed her; for the better. My younger self's initial impression of her was based entirely on her sexy image. Nothing more.

My encounter with a starlet from my youth led me to a guitar riff that would dramatically alter an old song—one I used to call 'Don't You Go There'. In the revised version, which ultimately became a Syato track to open an album, I put a femme fatale character—that was inspired by an urban legend once shared with me by Chris Datijan—at the centre. The story involves the wife of a Filipino worker in Saudi Arabia. The hapless husband is said to be spending time with friends one night after work, watching a triple X video. Intriguingly, the clip isn't scripted but a real tryst between a European guy and his Filipina love conquest. To his shock he realizes that the woman in the video is his wife whose lover secretly videoed their intimate episode. He and his friends are watching his wife being screwed, and who knows how many men have already seen the same thing!

The poor husband loses his mind and the woman, crowing in shame and guilt, jumps off a building, or so the unconfirmed story goes. Sounds too tragically cinematic to be true, huh? Yet, I was disturbed by it enough for me to take the title of the apparent Betamax tape containing the sex video. It was called 'Jeddah Queen'.

With the riff and storyline in my head, I composed the song free from the clutches of the pop genre—the call of the day—in the first Syato CD. This one's a part-new wave, part-alternative rock track containing the line 'fooled, humiliated by some asshole'. I had no plan of lobbying the song to any radio station. My wife thought that the first line—'You're the greatest who came out on screen'—directly addressing the woman with an intriguing moniker is arresting. There goes the double entendre.

'Jeddah Queen' does not have a chorus; its melody tries not to be repetitive. It's almost like a free verse if we take it as poetry. I don't recall having a hard time arranging the melody runs. The song just flowed once I had a clear idea of what I would write. There was no mention of someone dying by suicide. Yet, listening to the track, you know there's something tragic going on. The intro lines were an afterthought, like it came in my head unrelated to the rest of the song. Somehow, I felt those lines had to be there at the beginning.

For all the gripping pain embedded in this cathartic track I must say, it opened with some hope. 'Hello how are you today / I hope to help you get away / I know you might be hurting now / I wish to heal you somehow'.

Its intro made me decide it should open the album we were making, a follow up to Syato's all-Tagalog, self-titled debut album. If a listener moves quickly from the final song of the first album to 'Jeddah Queen', it's likely he'd not think that the albums were recorded under the same name. It was a total departure from our previous sound. I'm proud I was involved in both works.

Jeddah Queen's saga—as presented in our song—abruptly ends with a sudden stop, to stress some point. Towards that end note, you can hear me let out a far-out 'hey' to perhaps signal that the song is about to end. In live gigs, I would take the moment as an emotional release, like me telling the rest of the world, 'Come on, let me out'.

Sometime later I met a guy named Mike Lumba who's into remixing songs in electrohouse fashion. I sent him the track and he said he liked the guitar and bass work. As expected, he gave it his own danceable beat and repeated some lines for emphasis, in particular the line, 'Take off your clothes without your sin'. The result was an arrangement fit for a disco house, with rock elements. The introductory vocals were also cut off, so the version began with the riff.

One evening I was with Mike at a nightclub in Timog Avenue in Quezon City and he asked the DJ to play it. I saw some girls dancing to it.

Mike is a character; overweight when I first met him and talked really fast. He grew up in the US. One evening my brother Boygic and I treated him at a burger joint for dinner. My kuya and I amusingly witnessed how it took him just a couple of minutes to finish an American-sized burger. Years later, I saw Mike on social media, in way better shape and looking healthier. I felt happy for him. He could be dancing somewhere with those chicks who moved their bodies to the sound of electrohouse 'Jeddah Queen'.

Kaye and I find Mike real smart too. After the typhoon Ondoy wreaked havoc in Metro Manila and nearby areas, another storm came over. His post, 'Fuck, another one' floored us. It was the sort of thing a real cool dude would say.

I admit I was surprised he had trimmed down tremendously. Often it doesn't happen that an obese of his size goes as thin as he was able to. I tried to reconnect, but he was no longer responding. Some people are like that. They'll be around for one specific purpose and won't stick for whatever reason.

MCA Music, for a time, licensed Syato's second album tracks in digital format, including Mike's work for 'Jeddah Queen'. Partly due to miscommunication because of the pandemic, the tracks were automatically downed or erased from digital stores. Ivory Music, through their digital division Enterphil, re-uploaded the tracks, but not including Mike's own touch of 'Jeddah Queen'. Yet, I'm confident it will one day resurface. That's the beauty of recorded music. It will come out one way or another.

Chapter 6

Minor Hit

It still breaks my heart that I could not score my first legit hit despite my efforts. My wife, Kaye, has tried her best to caress my wounded heart by reminding me from time to time that one of my songs was actually a minor hit.

The Syato track 'Tibo' did earn an airplay on Philippine mainstream radio back in 2009. It even reached the second spot in a provincial countdown by Radyo Natin, a station operated by the Manila Broadcasting Corporation (MBC).

That same year my son, Ryde, was born. I ended the first decade of the new millennium on a high note.

My spouse's unconditional love made her use the phrase over and over. A life partner stands by the other person no matter what. She does know what I mean when I say legit hit. It's that song that people sing along to and know by heart. I also understand her need to remind me of the blessings that come my way, which she says I tend to overlook.

In one of our nasty marital arguments, she only had to ask one question that shut my mouth off and reduced me to the littlest version of myself. *'May hit song ka?'* (Do you have a hit song?) she asked in a way you wouldn't want to hear.

Don't judge her. She wouldn't say something like that if I hadn't crossed the line. At times when I am frustrated, I am not able to control my lips from saying stuff best kept unsaid. I can confidently say that I deserved to hear that insulting remark from the woman, my wife, who has supported me since day one. Besides, there's really no point crying over your inability to score a hit. There will always be factors as to why a song can't hit its full potential. I'd also like to add that 'Tibo' is not even among my compositions I'd sing in my head from time to time. I didn't spend much time writing it. It took less than an hour to write the whole thing.

I was led to writing it and it had to be written. Mark told me about his co-worker, who was a lesbian and who looked prettier than most people at the Starbucks outlet where he worked during that time. The idea inspired the line *'Ang pogi ni Tibo, nakakatibo'* (The lesbian looks handsome, I'm attracted) and it became the song's hook.

I can't recall if it was a band decision to pick the song when our friend Espie Eusebio, a known radio promo specialist who led me to radio and record label people, asked for a song she could audition to Love Radio, which was the leading FM station.

Before we knew it the popular station was already playing it. One of its top DJs, Papa Jack, included it in his evening program rotation. Mark would even exchange text messages with him. One time I heard the DJ say on air, *'Sabi ni Mark, bokalista ng Syato . . .'* (Mark, the vocalist of Syato, said . . .).

Labelled as a rock novelty, 'Tibo' took Syato to some places and allowed us to gain a level of recognition. Years later, a young man named Ferdie Salamat told me that he used to cover my bass lines as heard on the track. He's the percussionist for a band whose foreign singer I interviewed and wrote about. He later became a friend and even joined my later band The Pub Forties in one of our TV guestings.

The 'Tibo' bass part is a simple groove that becomes the song's foundation. A slower run of it helped prep us up each time before launching ourselves into the song for most of our live gigs, especially when we toured Padi's Point outlets in August and

September of 2009 to promote it. It was always the last number considering its status as a radio release piece.

One afternoon, someone called up from FILSCAP and said I have an unclaimed cheque. I didn't know there was one. The amount on it he said was ₱64,0000 ($1,118). I found out that 'Tibo' had accumulated royalties based on the number of airplays it enjoyed during a certain time. The amount might be little for a hitmaker's royalty cheque, but I had never earned that big for a song I wrote. Victory!

Another cheque for the same song came much later with nearly the same amount. In short, I earned more than ₱100,000 ($1,748) for 'Tibo'. Certainly not bad for a song I didn't spend much time writing.

I still wonder why 'Scorpio', which also had radio airplay exposure, didn't amass quite the same royalty. Nevertheless, it meant two of my songs had fine FM radio runs.

To help push 'Tibo' further, we had a music video for it directed by acclaimed independent filmmaker Sig Sanchez who worked on the video for Sugarfree's 'Hari Ng Sablay'. The boy featured in that major hit was also the one tapped for our song; shot mostly in a restroom inside the building where Candid Records—distributor of Syato's second album *Sticking By*—was housed.

It was fun making that video and we were able to put in Mark's cousin Candy and my niece Bianca, as well as our drummer Macky's girlfriend. The name of my sister Beverly's unica hija was mentioned in an earlier Syato recording ('Elkyu').

'Tibo's' crowning glory came in December 2009 when our band performed at MYX Mo, an annual live spectacle of the most popular bands in town. We were the opening band in the pre-show, right after singer Gian Magdangal's number. It was an experience straight from a B-movie, with a sea of people in front of us and Mark going down to the crowd while singing the song. I thought we deserved a better billing but it is what it is. At least we were able to be on the MYX Mo stage, which around that time was the ultimate gig for an active band.

Album cover of Syato's sophomore album 'Sticking By' distributed by Candid Records in 2008. From left: JM Delos Santos, Erickson Villarmino, Mark Villagomez, Yugel Losorata, and Macky Brosas. (Images taken by Chito Cleofas)

Chapter 7

Baby Talk

As a songwriter, sometimes I come up with tunes inspired by something or someone cute. These tunes are meant to entertain children and pets. I am inspired by, say, comic characters or stuffed toys. I'd feel shy to let others hear them, except probably my wife and son.

I don't have any inhibitions humming these baby tunes for my wife and son to hear. It's part of our bond as a family, them seeing me child like.

Mark's son, Rhyme, my nephew, had once amused me with his attraction for outer space matters and under-the-sea creatures. As a toddler he liked planets and sharks. So, for him, I came up with this tune with the words, 'You're my bro barumbacaro'. The meaningless word just sounded right to me.

Our family's first dog, a poodle named Clooney, which was given to me as payment for PR (press relations) work once became my inspiration for a melody. I'd hum it when I was being playful with him. I'd imagine this random tune sounding like a dozen percussion instruments playing the same thing, with a nursery rhyme-like line that goes 'Bon-Bon-Bon-Clooney-Bon'.

I guess these cute pieces of music are manifesting my endearment towards children and little animals. These melody snippets capture the child in me. There's a part of me that can't grow old. Music is my avenue to keep my youth breathing. It belongs to my soul, to my existence.

My son, Ryde, is naturally a recipient of these little tunes that get into my head and won't let go. I have a nephew-in-law before who I describe as my practice child because he was the infant I could place in my arms prior to the birth of my own boy. His name's Dustine, the son of my wife's late cousin Emir who used to fondly call me 'bayaw' (brother-in-law). He was the only other person who'd call me bayaw apart from my real brother-in-law, Mark. Sadly, Emir didn't even reach forty. He struggled with liquor, even one time joking that since his father was downed by drinking, his goal was to empty all those beer and gin bottles as vengeance! Emir must have been proud that I like his child. I did feel he appreciated me for that.

My little melody for Dustine came when I named him Dustine Reboyo out of the blue. His surname's Mercado. Then I came up with this phrase for him, 'The last of the Reboys', which didn't make sense at all. Maybe I was thinking about the movie *The Last of the Mohicans*.

Unsurprisingly I'm drawn to the sound of the bass guitar so most of these baby tunes are driven by the bass groove. If I will turn them into real songs, it's likely that the bass will be featured prominently. 'Tas Batas' is a bass-driven melody line on a nickname we gave to Dustin for a time. Dust is Tas, Batas is Tagalog for law. They just rhymed together.

There are classic lyrics that don't make sense. In the Philippine music scene, that is best exemplified in the novelty hit 'Butsekik', popularized by Yoyoy Villame. He said that the words are store names, owned by Chinese traders, which he randomly put together. They don't mean anything at all. Same goes to the Spanish words put in by John Lennon in the Abbey Road track 'Sun King'. This technique shows the importance of the words and melody sounding good together.

Once I composed by putting a melody to the line 'Here I'm back to let you know that I'm still watching Cinderella tonight'. I didn't know why I chose those words and what they meant, but I'm sure it fitted the melody. In particular, the word Cinderella is perfect for it. As of this writing I haven't gone past that line to turn it into a full song I wish to call 'Here I'm back'. It is very unlikely that I will replace a set of words that has stuck with me.

My musical inclination reached a point of parodying a Beatles classic by changing its words. It struck a chord with my brothers at least when I sang something for one of us, Rockefeller, whom I called 'boss' for a time. It's about his girl schoolmate named Lorraine who lived near our house. The song is The Beatles' 'Hey Jude'. I altered the first verse line. It went, *'Hey bos, nandiyan si Lorraine. Nag-aantay sa kanyang bahay. Si Bea umuwi ka na Bea. Nang dumating si Lorraine. Umuwi ka na Bea'* (Hey boss, there's Lorraine waiting at her house. Bea, you go home. And then when Lorraine arrives, you go home).

Bea is the youngest among my siblings. The whole point of the line is that, when it says *'Umuwi ka na Bea'*, the voice does it on a high pitch. When it returns to the same line, the voice transforms into a macho voice. In effect, he needed to sound like a big, muscled man because his 'crush' had arrived. Pure childish fun. Me and my brothers, including Rockefeller, still get a laugh when I start singing it during reunion gatherings.

After deactivating in 2016, Syato briefly reunited prior to singer Mark Villagomez relocating to New Zealand. Also in photo is drummer Arly LaGuardia (second from left) who joined the group in 2010.

Chapter 8

Gift Rapper

As with the first Syato, while live performances provide instant gratification basically by way of audience applause, recording could be more fun if the process is going smoothly, and the musicians involved are working harmoniously. It's a big bonus if you have control over how things are done with the collaborative atmosphere being present. I can speak for that in 'Tulay', one of my co-writing efforts with rapper Blanktape, who I first met in a guest appearance on a music segment of a show hosted by another friend—Pin-Up Girls band leader, Mondo Castro.

During the taping we discussed controversial songs because Blanktape's hit song 'Banana' is thought to be lyrically obscene. Our band Syato's 'Tibo' is part of the conversation due to its link to lesbianism.

I can't recall how heated the discussion, but the comical and street-smart Blanktape appeared cool; he primarily carried the episode. He was talkative, putting extra life into the conversation. I was looking for a rapper-collaborator at the time and he fell right into my path.

We started with the song 'Bumbunan', a composition of mine about temper. The original line was '*Huwag mong ilagay ang init ng kalan sa yong bumbunan*' (Don't put the stove's heat on your head), which I came up with after I observed the flame on the stove one night while my wife was cooking dinner. I changed *'kalan'* (stove) to *'kamay'* (hand) and from there it was quick. I thought of two characters: Dino, a street jerk who met his match; Dina, a girl with a pretty face who is quick to anger. Nobody dares woo her. Blanktape supplied rap lyrics and it felt good the first time we jammed the song with him doing his bit.

Of the four compositions we collaborated on, three were largely my tunes and lyrics, but he put in valuable rap lyrics to contribute. One of them 'Alay Sa Mga Bigo' (Offering to the broken) had rap verses I actually wrote myself. It was my attempt to write a rap song and I owe it to Arlen Mandangan, Blanktape's real name, that he delivered the words on record with passion.

I'm most proud of the chorus to 'Alay Sa Mga Bigo', which I wrote while in Coron, Palawan riding in a motor boat, feeling the air blowing hard into my face. That felt cool as I watched over the open sea and the chorus tune coming out, as if whispered to me by the strong wind. Mark would one time comment so positively about it. He was assured that I composed a good singalong tune. On record we happily sang together with the rest of the group.

The song was remixed by Ferdie Marquez of the original True Faith line-up. He was the guy on guitar with a short chin, Bless his soul. He was a good guy and we may have collaborated further had he not died at fifty. I would drop by his condo unit for the song's mixing. Being the expert in what he does, he dropped the drums and keyboard and replaced a programmed drum track. It produced a better sound. At first, I felt uneasy that my initial bass line was too close to my playing on The Cure's 'Lovesong'. Ferdie retained it though to nice effect.

During one of our drinking sprees with Blanktape, he introduced a song called 'Sabi Mo'. It was already a complete song with his obligatory rap verses. In my mind it wasn't necessary to put more on it just for the heck of contributing. I also felt like giving back the favour to him after he rapped lyrics for 'Alay Sa

Mga Bigo'. It was also not an issue that he presented 'Sabi Mo' already as a full piece. I was happy to sing back up and help turn it into a Syato song.

Naturally, Blanktape was in command during the sessions for 'Sabi Mo'. I would make suggestions from time to time, but I knew where I stood. Back in high school when I was in the theatre group, our mentor Mrs Bumanglag said the line 'Know where you stand' so often that when I recall her each time I hear her voice say that. She said she had been yelled at by film director Joel Lamangan during her own time as a theatre student.

Since Arlen wrote 'Sabi Mo', I expected that the record had to sound to his taste. I was seated in the passenger seat with my wife who was driving when we heard the song come out of the radio. He pushed for it to get a few airplays and I appreciated that. Sadly, the track is no longer in digital stores after he had it pulled out, saying he'd want the song to be new again if and when someone records it. I don't get that really. It was a little bit of an affront considering the effort our group gave to rehearse and record the track. The track can still be heard on YouTube, by the way. Again, I just had to tell myself that I know where I stand. I cannot spend too much time fighting for a song I didn't write.

But rest assured that I had no regret doing collaborative work with Blanktape. It was a lot of fun writing and recording with him. The peak of our partnership could be heard on 'Tulay', which originally came out in his album *Sana'y Mapansin* in 2013. Eight years later, I finally saw the track released under the Syato with Blanktape name, dropped in digital format. Before that, the song was included in a compilation where our band wasn't even credited as co-artist. Such omission is part of small band problems.

'Tulay' as a composition is important to me. It is based on a real-life experience, the consequence of asking for a friend to help woo a classmate in second year college. The girl and my ex-friend ended up falling for each other and even had a child of their making. I was too broken-hearted at the time, I shut off my pal and told him we could no longer be friends. By the time I wrote the piece, the experience had become a source of laughter for me. With Blanktape's entry and him coming up with the narrative rap portraying my old pal's role, the song transformed into a pop rap reggae with a novelty touch to it. The funny plot fitted the feel of the song, and I enjoyed playing the bass especially in the verses where I had gone to my instrument's higher register to produce a deeper sound. My bass line appeared to me like I was bullying my pal while he was trying to explain his position. I let my bass retaliate back.

Mark Villagomez sang on the track well too. He was able to inject his specialty of the house, the growl, at the climax. As a cute footnote, we recorded Ryde's voice saying 'Hindi pwede' (not allowed) and 'What you say?' as those were his expressions when he was about four. It suited well leading to the final exchange between Mark and Blanktape where they revealed they wouldn't resort to a fistfight to settle the score. Well, I can say I'd do the unthinkable, that is forgive my screwer, if I get to see him again. I'd make peace with him. As I have said that episode is now just another funny memory from my youth. Back then I had to drop the idea of going to journalism major because the girl was going to the same class. I regretted that immature decision.

Chapter 9

Interview with a Rock Star

Interviewing famous musicians can at times be a daunting task. Part of me is screaming that I should have been in their league too. Yes, I am a legit fan of some of them whose work I have admired through the years, but in the back of my head, I see them as people who just earned a break and have been—or should be—enjoying the perks.

A few of these breakthrough acts are to me overrated and acting prima donna.

One time inside the conference room of a record label, I was interviewing this famous rock band when I sensed they were answering my questions in an intentionally stupid way, and they would laugh after finishing their childish antics. I couldn't be wrong. They were making me feel like I was asking dumb questions. They were not seriously answering them. I came there to do my work and I had to go through the terrible traffic of Metro Manila to do a job that I love. Why can't a supposed rockstar give an answer to a question that fans also want to ask?

I asked a rocker his thoughts about reuniting with his old band for the sake of their fans and he almost walked out on me. If I don't ask such a question I will be criticized by their anticipating hordes of supporters or my editor, who would call my attention for not asking the right question. Why show attitude if you can be polite? Some people choose to be mean when it's easy to be kind. For a second, I thought I was going to have a fistfight with the rest of his bandmates in the room. No match. I surely would have gone to heaven with a black eye if that happened!

If you think about it, no one should be entitled to act like a dick, regardless how big a star is, or even if it's human nature to get some air of pride and feel like the world owes you its joy.

One evening I asked a quartet a serious question right after they performed in one of those well-attended MYX MO Live, only to be greeted with an off the cuff remark after its bassist said he thought some of the girls around were fuckable. The other three actually didn't laugh at it. My head was like, 'If only I could hit this guy and tell him his bass lines are not that remarkable for him to talk that way . . .'

I can't be blamed for trying my best not to be a pushover opposite these so-called rockstars. It's essential to survive. You allow them to do that once or twice and you bet they will brand you as someone they can step on and who will not fight back. I recall a colleague once told me that I cannot be intimidated by the mean artists because I am an artist myself.

In many instances I refrain from asking slambook questions. I feel like I need to send the message that I know what they're doing and the kind of life they've been through prior to fame. Sometimes an interviewee would have a gut feeling that I am a musician, too, which makes me feel more connected.

I find it phony when band members sit in an indoor press con wearing shades. Unless the sun is asking you to wear one, you have to take them off, especially during a one-on-one interview. For the one asking the questions, conversing with someone wearing dark glasses is like being watched by a voyeur via a one-way mirror. It's disrespectful. It's not my problem if you have an eye bug or your eyes are red from drug abuse. I deserve the courtesy of being allowed to make eye contact with the person I'm going to write about. I believe I am a journalist who can move on to the next interviewee if the prior one doesn't have spare time for me.

If your purpose is to look cooler than the person interviewing you, that's way too cheap. I spend time and money getting to the venue. My ears sometimes bleed due to the awful music I have to endure. So, the least a rockstar can do is think that the journalist in front of him is doing him a favour. I won't be less of a human being if I don't get to interview a particular musician. A better, or kinder for that matter, artist is right 'round the corner. I go to press cons to do my job professionally and be of help to artists' cause. I'd rather play my own music than hear a stupid answer.

I feel for entertainment journalists who find themselves at the other end of a sarcastic reply from rock stars thinking they're being asked silly questions. I do see the frustration that creeps when you have to answer such commonly asked questions while you're preparing for or steaming off after a show. But that doesn't give you the right to be harsh. A rocker doesn't deserve to be featured if they think of the entertainment press as chiefly spreaders of gossip. One's ethics is necessary in moments like press interviews.

Journalists have their moods too. There will be times when they might be caught flat-footed. At the end of the day, they will still write about you. It shouldn't be too much to provide a decent answer to questions that have to be asked. There's nothing personal when a journalist asks a personal question. It's part of the job, part of the press con that helps make an artist look extra interesting.

Artists who made it have to remember that fame may fade, but a journalist can keep their spot until he writes thirty. You have to be appreciative of someone who'd make an effort to keep you relevant or appearing in the news.

I won't allow a rock star to swat me for I know in many ways the music scene is unkind to my bands. When provoked I'm ready to vent my own frustration on someone acting improperly or making use of their stature as an excuse to be angsty. Fame should make you humble and low-profile as you're given the power to inspire others. How can one be inspirational if they're showing a bad attitude towards people, including journalists?

My bands have experienced being interviewed by members of the media and never did we act with attitude. I, myself, always smile while the interview's happening and make the interviewers feel that I'm genuinely interested in talking to them.

Since I'm often the one explaining the origin of our band's name or how we began as a group, I'd do a lot of the talking and I make sure that I don't appear as if I'm trying to be smart. It's easy. I only need to answer the questions correctly, sincerely, and politely. Those are the three things an interviewee must do, regardless of whether a question is a bit dull, or too intriguing, or way overboard. You can still respond to an inappropriate question with a kind word, and make the interviewer feel that their tactic is not working.

The writer-musician with his basketball player-son Ryde for whom he wrote the digital single 'Next Big Thing'

Chapter 10

Renditions

In my years in the music beat, one of the more noteworthy topics to discuss is the innate power that an original version of a song possesses. Original in this context is the recording that officially introduced a song to the listening public and became famous for that matter. Nothing beats the original, we hear people say.

The classic 'Stand by Me' by Ben E. King has been re-done countless times. Yet the airy and fresh feel of the fifties recording, with its simple big bass-dependent structure, remains definitive. Same as 'Imagine' or 'Yesterday' where several singers, some even more technically gifted than either John Lennon or Paul McCartney, tried to sing them better, but couldn't.

On a positive note, some of these cover acts weren't attempting to outdo the original counterpart at all. They're trying to give the songs some new flavour. I heard a member of a local band doing a live gig at Hard Rock Café informed the bar crowd that their bass player's version of 'Yesterday' is, at least for them, better than the work of Paul. I did hear their rendition and there was no way it's better than how Macca's voice delivered his most important composition. I'm not even thinking of the master recording that appeared on *Help*, but the raw first take taped for other Beatles to listen to, which graced *The Beatles Anthology 2*.

Someone must already be too drunk to even let out such a claim!

There are instances though that a cover beats the original recording. Natalie Imbruglia's 'Torn' is a revival few may know. Her version is easily more radio friendly than the first version released, with clean sounding strumming and a bass line comfortably enjoying the party, not getting in the way of the other elements in the instrumentation. It became her signature hit.

Nirvana's live take of David Bowie's 'The Man Who Sold the World' turned the song on its head. The world bought their version, especially Kurt Cobain's viscerally felt vocals.

Arguably a cover version is better simply because the original didn't become a monster hit. That makes a big single essentially untouchable. It's a disrespect to try to outdo Michael Jackson's 'Billie Jean'. Even MJ himself couldn't top his first take on the song! That take one vocal is the way we've been hearing it since it came off the historic *Thriller* album.

Having said that, the logic of covering a popular song is to give it a new life, a different interpretation that veers away from how it's done as everybody knows it. When an audiophile finds a twist unique and interesting enough from the original to earn repeat listens, then the singer is able to successfully deliver a fine rendition. Chris Cornell has his version of 'Billie Jean', which is way different from MJ's style.

According to my wife, Kaye, it is only upon hearing Cornell's version that the song's message appeared crystal clear to her. Something in his voice tells with emphasis that the kid is not the singer's son.

But hey, it doesn't mean the late rock star triumphed over MJ's groundbreaking moonwalking. Kaye agreed. She just appreciated the way the iconic Soundgarden frontman bravely delivered the song.

Needless to say, 'Billie Jean' will always be the King of Pop's crowning moment.

My composition 'Sandalan' was rendered by Noela Amparo and the Apat Band in a lounge feel version on purpose, after a radio station thought that their released recording sounded too noisy. Some friends easily fell for the more calming version. Later I was told that the producer of Noela's record of 'Sandalan' prefers that she performs the song in pop rock style. He's apparently a lover of upbeat tracks. The message was clear; the matter is subjective in nature.

'Sandalan's' fate will be sealed once mainstream listeners embrace it in whatever version. I understood Noela when she insisted that she liked to interpret the song the way she did it on the demo. She's not going to mimic Angel Andal's original release interpretation, which is the proper thing to do. When you hear someone sing a song the way it is done by the artist who popularized it, that one is not hell-bent on leading a career in recording. It's either they are part of a showband rendering the latest craze in a live bar, or just some artists trying hard, yes, 'second-rate copycat' showing off via a karaoke machine.

I've been seeing synth-flavoured or lavishly produced '80s songs reinterpreted with only acoustic guitar or minimal accompaniment. Such versions show how beautiful those '80s songs are melodically, as revealed through stripped-down performances. My appreciation of Cutting Crew's 'I Just Died in Your Arms' came in full throttle when I saw on YouTube its singer-composer performing the classic with just a guitar and his stylish, seducing vocals during a concert. It made me pick an acoustic guitar and sing it myself.

I'm sticking to my belief that if a song has a beautiful melody, you can interpret it in various ways and chances are you will get the same favourable result. Eighties music is often devalued for its apparent pretentiousness in terms of sound production. But if we think about it, a large number of tracks from that era can match or even surpass those from other decades with just its basics.

Showbands are not as respected by the listening public in general because they're known to just copy the hits. It's really not that they don't have originals, they're just less focused on exploring the idea of making originals. They're busy sticking to the *plakado* (playing a song as it is popularly known, note for note) rule. They don't make their own versions partly because patrons want to enjoy the hits the way they're used to hearing them.

Sure, the bar dwellers dance to the imitation. On the other hand, if you give them a beautiful alternative take, it may surprise and excite them more. Copying a song can provide outright appreciation. Yet, a cover well thought out and presented, even though may initially be met with scepticism, eventually emerges as a pleasant reroute worth going to.

When The Cure's 'Lovesong' was covered by 311 in reggae form, and was thus slower in tempo, other bands covering the song began doing the same thing. I often insisted to my bands that we do that song in Cure's style, and then I found out that I've been playing the notable bass line quite different from how it is on the original record. Being in bands with more original tracks, as opposed to being in a full-time cover band, pointed me to the direction of routinely coming up with something on my own.

Chapter 11

Rebirth

With life's fragility in the face of failures and mortality, embracing the essence of rebirth is a must to absorb the feeling of rejuvenation. That's a better option than accepting defeat or death. Every time I'd have this good feeling, it was like being back in my youth, overwhelmed by the feeling of your entire future waiting ahead of you. You may say it's mere daydreaming, but the feeling amounts to the good vibe that can help you last another lifetime.

The re-release of Syato's *Sticking By* album, this time in digital music stores, felt like a new lease on life for our band that had gone inactive back in 2016. The positive vibe it provided was a morale boost.

So what if the record was thirteen years old in reality? It was technically new in the realm of music online. Nearly none of today's listeners have gotten hold of the CD that featured the tracks originally released, from back when physical CDs were still the format used to get your music out.

With that in mind I was hoping one of the tracks would fall into the new songs' playlist.

That June in 2021, lady luck smiled and the album's opening track, 'Jeddah Queen' landed on both Spotify's Fresh Finds Philippines list and Apple Music's Absolute OPM. It was indeed a rebirth of sorts. It gave me satisfaction that perhaps the latest generation of listeners was about to embrace my band's music, and my compositions.

Sticking By was personally special considering that all ten tracks were my compositions. I only had to pick ten of my existing compositions at that point. It proved to be a once-in-a-lifetime privilege. I'm not saying I won't find a way to make that happen again, but the circumstances and mindset I'm living with make it hard to duplicate such a feat.

Come to think of it, I may have been one of the few artists in the band scene who really was able to do the trick. It's quite a validation of my leadership and determination as a band person, regardless of if that matters or not to even people I know. I've learned to be happy within. I have no control of people's minds. My control is basically limited to what I can produce.

While 90 per cent of the content of *Sticking By* had been released previously by MCA Music, that digital release was with a couple of new, original tracks. The album was presented in different packaging, with a reshuffled song sequence and a new title.

The album in its original form had been put out in the digital realm by Ivory Music, which happens to be the same label that financially backed Syato's debut CD. A new horizon appeared out of the sky.

I hardly saw the sky at the height of Covid-19 pandemic, by the way. I was practically locked up at home or working remotely as copy editor for *CNN Philippines*.

There was no fanfare for the *Sticking By* re-release. The pandemic made sure there was no reunion jam for the Syato line-up that kept the group active for some years, way longer than the first line-up. There was a bit of interest from curious listeners. But more than anything, it was bliss for me knowing that the album was now accessible through digital stores. It revitalized my deep affection for Syato—from the original line-up to the last set of personnel to perform as Syato.

There had been a point when I was trashing whatever Syato did because I was so into my new band, and I didn't want to be reminded of its failures. I was hell-bent on correcting my supposed past mistakes and to do this, I felt like I had to turn my back and sort of belittle my former band's accomplishments or call it whatever. It was a way of facing my demons and going through the pain of deactivating a group I went to war with for long.

I saw an interview of Ely Buendia wherein he was asked about what the Eraserheads meant to him, and his reply was a stoic, 'Banda ko . . . dati' (My band, before). Many people may have found that answer wanting and tantamount to discrediting the massive achievements of his ex-band. I believe it was just a manifestation of the hurt of letting go of an important aspect of someone's life.

On a personal note, Syato can never be just a former band of mine. It is a band I fought for and tried everything in my power to carry somewhere. 'Jeddah Queen' being labelled as a 'fresh find' is short of saying it is new.

A revival song gives the original release a fresh run. An album that was put out for limited copies surely has the right to enjoy the luxury of reaching netizens from all walks of life. Listeners only need to have the proper gadget and access to song distribution apps.

My brother-in-law, Mark Villagomez, had already relocated to New Zealand, and we were not the type of band that would record remotely. We were used to being in the same room and laying in our individual parts in the presence of everyone else.

Even if Syato can't be resurrected, *Sticking By* reborn was a step in the right direction.

If there is one thing I've learned from being in a band in the Philippines, even if there is struggle most of the time, it is to count the little victories I came across, and maybe blow them up in my head as major triumphs. You do that when looking at small wins in a proper perspective. How many of us are able to record music, go around gigging, do a radio or campus tour, write songs with friends, write about other musicians and music, and write about your own true-to-life tale of passion, pain, perseverance, and parties? (These are parties in the form of evening gigs, recording sessions, press conferences, and songwriting exercises with or without a partner).

Counting blessings is a path to feeling less a loser and more a winner. I'd like to believe that if I've struggled a lot, it's not because I suck.

Some musicians have the skill and determination but are not valued enough due to political and social reasons, like some of those unsigned, unheard, playing underground or in their garage, and who are keeping themselves intact while trying to score the big break. I sleep well knowing I have done the best I could, with the help of friends, family, and a handful of fans to pull things off. Essentially, it's okay to be underrated as long as you earn the respect of the lovely few who manage to stop and carefully listen to your music.

Chapter 12

Third Album that Never Was

Syato technically produced two full-length albums, along with a number of non-album songs that may be packed into a separate album, though the span of time covering the release dates of these latter songs stretched to fourteen years. There's even less cohesion among the songs considering that something you have recorded five years ago may likely be so different from what you're about to put onto tape.

I was hoping for a third album under the Syato catalogue to complete a sort of trilogy. We tried but it didn't work out.

Sometime in the first half of the 2010s, Syato came into the Manila home of my old friend Nolit Abanilla, the same guy who helped The Dreamers produce a demo years ago. Nolit had been championing indie artists for years and Syato being unsigned (by a record label) found home under his care.

We recorded a number of songs, and we enjoyed the process. One day JM came to Nolit's place by himself and recorded some guitar parts for a composition of mine called 'Pagsapit Ng Unos'. When I dropped by a few days after, I was thrilled by what I heard. I loved the riff he put at the intro so much that I asked Nolit to paste it in other parts of the song. The power of digital mixing!

Back in The Dreamers days we needed to replay parts we wanted in repetition. The technology back then was still primitive compared to what Syato now had access to.

'Pagsapit Ng Unos' was the lone track we recorded from that series of sessions with Nolit that actually became a single. Shelved for a few years, I had it released as a Syato track on the day Mark flew to New Zealand.

Mark sang the song with grit, and I played a keyboard part that felt effective amidst the mix of heavy guitars and Arly's playful drum rolls. Arly's style had been a point of discussion at times because he tended to play extra beats not appropriate for some songs. He's a good player and he only needs to calm down for the others to keep up.

I told Arly that the break in 'Pagsapit Ng Unos' needed just the kind of rolling he usually does. He happily played and the result was good and very Arly. It was my little nod to him, having replaced Macky and serving the group with intense dedication. Arly did not play in the two Syato albums, but his presence was a key aspect in why the group lasted for more than half a decade since the promotion for the second album ended.

Before the sessions with Nolit had wrapped up, he asked us to contribute a song for his compilation paying tribute to Filipino revolutionary hero Andres Bonifacio. The song we handed him was a collaboration between me and JM, called 'Saludo'. This one's the only collaborative piece that JM and I worked on. I wrote the verses quite easily after it came out to my head while playing a simple chord pattern. I handed it to JM who composed the refrain and chorus.

By this time, JM had blossomed as a songwriter in his own right. He wrote a piece called 'Hintay', a rock ballad that became part of our live set rotation, and a favourite of Mark.

On record, I couldn't resist putting my own back-up vocal line in the spaces in the verse that I felt needed some filling.

When I contribute to someone else's composition I see that it is not forced.

We were still in collaboration with Blanktape around that time and I was challenged to write a rap song. I came up with 'Alay Sa Mga Bigo.' It was a good exercise to write lyrics bound to be rapped. Naturally I asked Blanktape to deliver what I penned.

Hats off to him for doing it. He was not critical of my effort to compose a rap song.

A couple of years later I finally came up with a verse to fit the balladry of the chorus. I labelled it as the ECQ (Enhanced Community Quarantine) version as it was during that period—locked at home due to a digital age pandemic—that I wrote it down.

Something with how Ferdie Marquez reworked the song for digital single release made me decide to drop the third album idea and just release songs one at a time.

'Alay Sa Mga Bigo' was released in August of 2016. Syato was virtually no longer performing at the time. Prior to the sessions with Nolit, we recorded a few songs at the Amerasian Studio, the place where Viva Records produced records.

In 2011, my visits to the office of Philippine radio big boss Manny Luzon gave us the opportunity to record a couple of radio jingles. It put Syato in a fun situation of doing something that was assured to have airplay from 91.5 Big Radio.

With some lyric guidance from Mr Luzon, I composed 'Big Time' using a tune from my vault of unreleased melodies. The recording had real good vibes. I wish I could prolong the happy hours we spent inside the studio making this. I was on cloud nine providing a little bass line intro to send the song into the airwaves. It would make me smile when hearing the jingle on the radio.

The other jingle we recorded, for 107.5 Win Radio, briefly reunited me with RJ from the original Syato line-up. I asked him to sing parts of it with Mark, marking the only time that both Syato

lead vocalists were on the same track. It's also a song I pulled from
my scrapbook of tunes.

The recording of the two radio jingles came around the time
the band was finding a new direction after dabbling with Tagalog
pop and alternative rock. Doing jingles always reminds you that
you can do commercial music without being a sell-out.

Yugel with his wife Kaye and their son Ryde

Chapter 13

Creative Freedom

I'm a fan of the two-headed monster for a band leader. But in the revamped Syato, I was way older and more experienced than everyone else to even share leadership duties. On the bright side, the set-up opened doors for creative freedom in songwriting. Here are four songs from *Sticking By* that made me feel that music-making is liberating.

'Panaginip Lamang'—I wrote this song while I was in The Dreamers. With me making sure that Chris gets a co-credit, this composition became a Syato track. I wrote it after I had a wet dream, almost, featuring my high school crush who was about to give me a torrid kiss. Just before her lips touched mine, I heard my mother's voice, and I was sent back to reality. I needed to wake up for my 7 a.m. college class at UST. You'd think it's a scene from a comedy flick, but it happened for real, and it inspired me to write a song about it. Somebody heard this track and used it as the theme for the final episode of actress Kim Chiu's *Your Song* weekly TV romantic comedy anthology.

'Broken Tuesday'. New wave is a sound and style I've been attached to forever; ever since I was introduced to it by my late brother kuya Boygic, who tried to write a couple songs himself. When I started writing songs in the '90s, the guitar had already replaced the keyboard as the coolest instrument. Being loud and raw was a welcoming shift from the synth-driven '80s. Yet, in my head the riff of this piece yearned for a keyboard sound, and even the bass line is 80-ish. I feel that the verse melody is stronger than any chorus I could come up with. 'I used to feel', the opening words that felt right, sounded melancholic and guided the direction of the song. I had this crush in UST Political Science class who told me we could only be friends. It was a sunny, sad Tuesday, and I changed it to 'rainy' for impact.

'Kung Wala Ka Na'. The 2000s were the era of *pogi* (handsome) rock bands—those fronted by supposedly handsome men and playing ballad rock, with '*hugot*' or sentimental lines about romance and heartbreaks. I challenged myself to come up with one and 'Kung Wala Ka Na' was the result. I heard from Kaye that one of the proofreaders in the editorial section of *Manila Bulletin* was going through some tough times. He was torn between his lover and his wife. I had to sit down and pick my guitar. It felt okay to have made use of the word '*marahil*' (somewhat) and I opened the song with a chord pattern that was different from the verses and chorus, and which I repeated in the latter part of the track.

'Bighani'. Seldom do I arrange a song by beginning it with the chorus. This has it and it felt good when I transformed what was originally a bridge tune into an instrumental intro. To my ears, it gave more depth to the narrative of the verses. I was at a party and feeling bored and then this stunner suddenly entered the room. The moment she got through the door, my goal was to get her name and number. Too bad we didn't have a common friend and I'm not the type to corner a stranger to flirt with me. Sometime later I saw the girl leave. I went home frustrated and woke up the following morning still feeling disappointed, as if I lost my chance to meet my destiny. I held the guitar and it calmed me. Then I wrote this song.

Chapter 14

End of Play for Syato

I was an active member of Syato for a total of fourteen years, which is longer than the combined time I spent with The Dreamers and the band I helped establish after I knew there was no more Syato. While the significant personnel change necessitates separating their respective tales, Syato was for me a single continuous run—long and winding you may say.

There were many factors that finally put a stop to the band's run, the most telling of which was the fact that after the radio airplay enjoyed by 'Tibo', there wasn't a follow-up to it. We'd be hearing other Syato songs getting played on the radio from time to time, like 'Bighani' or 'Sabi Mo', but that wasn't enough to keep the momentum going.

Syato in the first half of 2010s was a band in search of identity. We collaborated with Blanktape for a total of four songs in what was a move inspired by Linkin Park's rap and rock tour de force. Blanktape was a rapper singing novelty songs. We also made the odd move of officially naming our collaboration as Blanktape-Syato, instead of Syato featuring Blanktape which made more sense. All those songs, 'Tulay', 'Bumbunan', 'Sabi Mo', and 'Alay Sa Mga Bigo' sound like our band's arrangements, with rap portions from Blanktape as tokens.

I just thought Blanktape deserved higher billing. None of my bandmates suggested that, as it was not about who's more popular, the band should come first, and the guest artist follows.

JM eventually developed as front man material. He started learning how to write and sing songs. His good looks were a given advantage. It felt good for our band when girls started reacting once he got noticed on stage. I couldn't really tell how that felt for Mark, but I know my brother-in-law has always been a fair and kind person. He was sincerely happy for JM getting a lot of the attention.

Mark, being my wife's brother, was actually a liability for him. Out of frustration, I would at times put the blame on him when things weren't going Syato's way, like when we couldn't hear people clapping loudly after a gig. I eventually regretted labelling him as someone lacking charisma. I was like an older brother bullying his younger sibling. It was my fault. Mark did his best with the role given to him. He truly loved Syato while he was on board. I was ungrateful on some occasions.

The tension between brothers-in-law escalated and it came to a point that Mark decided to leave the band. I can't recall his last gig with us. I want to remember the great gigs, like the one night when we played at the artists' lair, the Saguijo bar in Makati. We arrived early and started drinking. By the time we were on stage, we were a bit tipsy. I could see Mark singing and smiling. I knew that smile. He was nearly drunk. I was, too, and I was swaying a bit while playing.

But the good thing, though, we were so loose and jolly that we performed with tremendous energy. We felt the crowd was into us. It was a good set. I couldn't remember how we got home.

A couple of lead guitarists came after Erickson/Meng who, sad to say, had to go because he was being unprofessional in many gigs he had with us. His problem with punctuality was a major issue. On that last one, we were given a slot at the famous

UP Fair gig in Diliman. Meng was nowhere to be found and we were about to play. We asked to be pushed further in the order of artists coming up to perform. It was so stressful. Kaye was there to watch us. She gave birth to our child just a few days after.

We joked after that the stress caused by Meng led to her premature labour.

I think letting go of Meng was a wrong move. He would eventually mature. One thing was sure, he had the talent. His replacement was a nice man named Elmer Sandig who played great lead parts in the song 'Bumbunan', among my favourite Syato tracks, and our version of Jolina Magdangal's 'Laging Tapat'. His stint ended because he relocated to Sweden where he is now a happy family man.

Next was Jimmy Velasquez who was a good-enough player but loved to drink. He was instrumental in turning Syato into a group that liked to drink after a jam session or recording. Some bad things were waiting to happen resulting from that nightly drinking. I was beginning to feel like a carefree college boy at some point and it affected my writing routine. My high school chum Jason Pahati, a politician in his hometown, joined the band for a time and it worked for a while.

This was the period when I was writing for *Yahoo Philippines* and *The Philippine Star*. Having a byline is a responsibility. It's not enough that you can write articles for media outlets. You have to be a man of good reputation too.

After countless drinking sessions, Jimmy had to detach himself from us. We had a fallout. Some friends just pass by. At least for a time you were really good friends and enjoyed each other's company.

JM for a short time became Syato's lead vocalist. It's cringy to even think that I allowed that to happen. I wonder how it felt for my wife that his brother was no longer part of my band. She didn't confront me about it. All throughout Syato's years, Kaye was always putting my welfare over anything. That's the kind of wife she is. On some occasions I would feel she was struggling to tell me the bitter truth that Syato's not going to make it in the music scene beyond what we had already experienced.

There was one gig at a mall that featured JM on vocals, and we invited Meng to play guitars, with Arly on drums. It was the only gig that featured both Meng and Arly, which Mark and I thought was a potent combination. Meng was out by the time Arly came. Sadly, when it finally happened, Mark wasn't there any more. It only lasted for one gig.

Somehow, personal problems I was dealing with made it hard for us to get a gig. Something was lost with Mark's departure. It felt like we were back on the drawing board. I was feeling angry over the whole thing. One time, JM led the others in appearing at a gig without me. They went with it against my advice and reasoned they couldn't say no. I felt hurt by that. Without announcing it, I decided not to perform with Syato any more. There was no official date when Syato just ceased to exist. It was early 2016.

In 2019, when relationships had been restored like brothers who just kiss and make up without really telling each other, we decided to set a couple of reunion jams. Mark was about to fly to New Zealand, so we set a gig at a bar owned by Freddie Aguilar, the singer-songwriter behind the international hit classic 'Anak', who I got to interview and write about in my *Manila Standard* column, Touchbass. We invited a few friends. It wasn't our best performance, but we tried to perform as decently as possible. After we were done, we gave each other a hug. I thanked Mark and the rest for helping me keep Syato alive as long as it could.

I will always be proud of Syato's achievements, little as they were. I must say I learned a lot about the realities of life being part or the leader of the band.

Bridge: The Pub Forties

The Pub Forties at Warner Music Philippines office after signing a distribution contract in January 2017. From left: Vince Borromeo, Yugel Losorata, Aries Espinosa, and Kap Maceda-Agila

Chapter 1

Life Begins at Forties

There was no formal ending to Syato. I have a muddled memory as to when was the last gig or jam. We just didn't gather again. We didn't hate each other. Something had to be closed to open a new chapter.

That chapter actually began when I met Aries Espinosa who was writing for the *Philippine Daily Inquirer* when I saw him for the first time in the early 2010s. I was sent by *The Philippine Star* to cover the taping of a reality TV show to be shot outside of Metro Manila, and featuring actress Marian Rivera, a famous face who would become the star of a 2023 movie billed as the highest grossing Filipino film of all time.

It was fun interviewing Marian, of course. But more importantly, that media junket introduced me to Aries who was not used to covering the entertainment scene. I thought he was a business reporter. I was wrong; he was into arts too. Just minutes after we began chatting, I found out he was into music and he sings.

We jammed a couple of times just to try it out. It wasn't working. Aries was bringing people I couldn't get along with. But I did notice he really could sing. In a cool twist of fate, Aries was a key figure of that band in *Inquirer* I had heard about while convincing Joseph, yes that Monday morning in *Manila Bulletin* so long ago, that we should form one ourselves.

In the summer of 2016, Aries and I jammed with drummer Kap Maceda-Aguila. Aries knew Kap as a motoring journalist. They were both on the same beat.

I met Kap at one of the press conferences he attended featuring visiting foreign concert acts. I recall he likes the band Jane Addiction and could play the drums. I remembered and invited him to jam with us.

At the time there was an original song I wanted to record and had even introduced it to Syato before the band's dissolution. The song was 'Road Rage', a bass line-anchored song inspired by my encounter with a violent man whom I witnessed hitting a woman inside a parked cab. I was a college boy walking home at night. On impulse, I slammed the car with my hand and that made the man stop what he was doing. He ran out of the car and chased me. I discovered that I can run quite fast in situations like that.

I suggested to Aries and Kap that we record 'Road Rage' to see how we would sound on record. They okayed and asked for a band name. That same night I thought about parodying the famed Beatles label—Fab Four—and came up with The Pub Forties. They liked it.

Not even one gig in, we went to Sonic State studio, one of the respected recording hubs in Manila where hit records had been made, including Orange & Lemons' Big Brother theme song 'Pinoy Ako'. On paper I wrote about the studio and its owner Jonathan Ong whose industry reputation was attested by the artist community. One night we were laying the guitar parts for 'Road Rage', Jon came into the studio and volunteered a guitar riff for the song that he said was running in his head. He was hearing what was going on inside. The riff he offered by playing it himself ended up on the record, right at the intro.

Punch Liwanag, the Ivory marketing guy who was with us on the day Syato signed a recording contract joined the sessions to supply the lead parts. He did a good job, and we used his practise take for another song because it had the right feel. For a while, we considered making Punch the band's official guitarist, but he declined because he was too busy with work.

The universe will always conspire with you. Around the same time, I bumped into Vince Borromeo at a mall. We met a long time ago when he attended Syato's launch of *Sticking By* at Padis Point in Cubao, Quezon City. I knew he used to be a recording artist as part of a duo. He writes songs, plays the guitar, and sings. We had a formal meeting to convince him to join the club of print media writers as he had been contributing to a broadsheet up until that point.

Aries took the lead in getting our first gig. It happened at an event for and by vegetarians. He was one of them. Event host RJ Ledesma, who had become popular as a commercial model, introduced us before we started playing. We heard him announce our band's name. I felt goosebumps as it dawned on me that I was part of a new band, again. We played a few covers, including The Beatles 'We Can Work it Out'. And then our original. 'There was a road rage / She ran away out of his car . . .' Aries sang. I was wearing a white polo. I felt some jitters. Aries was in his element. Kap appeared cool. I had to pull in a former Syato member, Meng, to play guitar for the occasion.

A new musical outfit of journalists had been born and Warner Music Philippines handed us a record distribution contract on January 31, 2017.

The Pub Forties during the shoot of 'Kay Sarap' music video in September 2022, orchestrated by Philippines-based marketing agency Blckmrkt. Also in photo is James Casas (third from left) who became the band's drummer by 2018

Chapter 2

How to Pick a Bandmate

There is really no formula for finding the best bandmates.

The most basic tip I can give is to look for people who can really play, and you can actually play with. If you're salivating for a guitarist who can handle the guitar a la Eddie Van Halen or a drummer who can hit the snare like John Bonham, you may end up being their groupie instead of a collaborator. John Lennon met Paul McCartney after a church ground gig of his pre-Beatles band The Quarrymen. Paul had been friends with George Harrison, whom he asked to audition to John. It was George then who reportedly suggested that they replace Pete Best with Ringo Starr whose drumming prowess he witnessed during a soundcheck.

Aries, Vince, and I struck it out as long as we could as Kap wrote a formal letter and emailed it to us to say he was quitting the band. At a bar gig in Resorts World Manila, a year after we released our first digital single, we asked someone to sit for him. We were just done performing when we found his letter!

For a time, Arly from Syato played for The Pub Forties, but he couldn't get along with our one-time guitarist Manny Tocol. We had a drink about it and he said he's leaving.

James Casas, a session drummer who earns by driving his car for rent, was recommended to fill in for him. James can play. He wasn't showy in his playing, and his nature to just play along to a song benefited The Pub Forties. Cool-to-be-with, humble, and a devoted family man, he easily blended with our personalities. You will never find him acting weird like most moody artists do. He saw things as they are and was never confrontational. He also has roots in the province of Masbate where my mother grew up and finds that detail an extra point to establish our friendship.

While Aries and I have always been intact since day one, Vince Borromeo was a really good pick for us to solidify as a band. He was a steal of the draft-type. Seldom can you find someone who provides a special flavour into the mix and purely enjoys his place. He is driven, representable, good-natured, and there's nearly nothing that makes him a liability.

The four of us—Aries, myself, Vince, and James—got closer and there was really a good vibe going around when we four were together either via a video call on messenger app or in person. It wasn't hard to pull everyone in when we felt it was time to jam face to face again.

Back in the day I felt Chris Datijan was bound to be special the first two hours after we were introduced. It was chemistry at first sight so to speak. I wasn't wrong. We spent the next six years of our lives, of our youth, playing and making songs together. That we could sit down together, face each other, and share melodies and lyrics throughout afternoons was definitely special. What we had was a rare occurrence.

But first there must be the connection that starts, whether it be from sharing the same corner in the office or at a bar. Often having similar orientation in music is a source of a spark. Being of the same age is surely a plus. How exciting it is to be talking to someone who grew up in the same era as you. I've had lengthy discussions with James about '90s bands and we could almost place ourselves back in time together.

Personality clashes can't foster band dynamics. Chances are you'd throw punches instead of creative ideas. Vince would sometimes talk about a particular topic that's beyond the scope of our ongoing discussion. But I am sure to get a thing or two from what he puts on the table. We're both writers and I believe we're on the same wavelength. Aries loves to inject punchlines to end a thought. I would find them laughable for their wit. Like-minded people may have transformed into bandmates more than heads all wanting to be the boss. It's all about finding those people with the same feathers.

Pun intended, you have to play it by ear when assessing someone if they are fit enough to be your bandmate or if you can bear to be in the same space playing through a set of chords for hours on end.

Chapter 3

Thank God It's New Music Friday

Spotify's New Music Friday playlist became a source of pride for artists whose new releases were picked by the platform's editors. A record's inclusion is taken as a validation that it got the attention of credible ears screening countless new releases. It gives a new digital single the exposure it needs to pull curious people into the song.

For a songwriter not used to getting into the charts, I appreciate that I made it to the list five times, so far.

Three of my compositions that made it were recorded by The Pub Forties: 'Drive On', 'Stop the World', and 'Next Big Thing'.

A composition with a special spot in my heart, 'Drive On' gave me the experience of landing on the playlist for the first time. I wrote the 2018 single in a room at Manila's Trader's Hotel where Kaye and I had checked in, courtesy of one of our ninangs at our wedding. I wrote it one morning after. The bliss of lovemaking and playing an acoustic guitar I just purchased gave me a smooth ride to coming up with a song about drive and driving along. Kaye always had a good perception of the song and I believe the group recorded it well under the guidance of Sonic State audio studio.

The ever-reliable Not Vinzons, Sonic's chief engineer and lead guitarist of the hit band Letter Day Story, played the ukulele to fade out the track using the instrument given to me by Uncle Gene, brother of my mother-in-law, Joy, who himself is a brilliant, self-taught musician. It was my idea, but I was still trying to learn how to play it, so I gave in when Not offered to do it himself.

I recall our distributor, Neptune Publishing, informing me about the accomplishment. I felt happy for our band. With digital streaming being the young generation's lot, 'Drive On' was somewhat our testament that age is not an issue when the music speaks for itself. You can still rock and roll even in your forties!

'You got to read all the signs right / Keep an eye on every road,' the song says.

As a songwriter, recording and releasing a composition is one thing. The song getting some acclaim is another. For one week I was messaging or telling people around that The Pub Forties song could be found on the special playlist.

We got busy as a result. We played in company parties and book launches and we got invited to a music festival in Cavite and as far as Cagayan De Oro where we fronted for Joey Ayala and Dong Abay. The band visited my brother's wife's place where we were treated to a hefty meal by their padre de familia. My brother was working in Dubai at the time.

It took a year and a half since 'Drive On' was released before we could come out with a follow up. We waited quite long for the right song. 'Stop the World' was released in August 2019 and once again the group made it to Spotify's New Music Friday.

The track featuring our Swedish friend Jeanette Kamphuis on violin is so far the most streamed Pub Forties track, even if the number is only a few grains in a sea of salt. The song is technically a revival piece since the boy group Voizboys did its original recording for their only album release. I prefer The Pub Forties version, with the violin heightening its emotional grasp to class. I also liked the fact that my bass part sounded big and round, and I have kept loyal to the way I played it during the early Syato/Staffbox days.

Interestingly we got invited to play at the *Manila Bulletin* lobby in Intramuros where a stage had been set up for invited artists to play. It was a sort of homecoming for me, and I was warmly greeted by former officemates. I certainly liked the air that day. They seem to be telling me that I've gotten a long way from the newbie writer picked to fill up a slot.

In a cute twist we had to play 'Stop the World' and Ronald Jayme, the old Syato vocalist who first heard the song when we jammed it in the early days of our band, was there to witness. He remained with the *Bulletin* after leaving Syato.

Chapter 4

Something Called 'Sandalan'

My composition 'Sandalan' had the distinction of being both a track I was tasked to deliver and a song that came out of thin air. I was feeling such air in a rehearsal studio one Saturday morning. It was a studio built inside the house of a real estate developer whom I became friends with after I wrote about a band he put up and whose songs he composed. When that group disbanded, he asked me to help him form one, and offered his rehearsal room. I pulled in Syato boys Arly La Guardia to play drums and Jimmy Velasquez, who became our lead guitarist after Meng's departure, to handle guitar duties. Our troika was meant to back a young female singer.

One Saturday in 2013, prior to leaving our condo unit in Victoria Towers in Timog Avenue in Quezon City for a scheduled jamming session, I saw my wife, Kaye, weeping on my way out. It had to do with her resigning from *Manila Bulletin* after she was transferred from the entertainment section to a beat she was not used to covering. She felt it was time to move on. But of course, it was natural to feel sad about dropping something you love.

Seeing her cry, my heart was instantly broken to pieces. I had to vent my anger on music as I walked out of the house frustrated and couldn't look back at her in tears. Our *Bulletin* days were officially over. Back in 2005, the year we tied the knot, I shifted from employee status to freelancing so she could stay because company policy does not allow married employees.

Inside the rehearsal studio, while we were running through a set of chords that I felt sounded strong, I suddenly blurted out a melody with made-up words to go by. The words were '*Di ko papayagang . . .*' That line led to the whole song. I asked Arly and Jimmy that we keep jamming with the same chords (G#-Eb-C-C#) as I flesh out the chorus melody. When we took a break, the song had a verse and the chorus. I only had to connect the verse to the chorus. I felt I had a good song going as I ate pizza.

After a week we were introduced to a girl named Noela Amparo who tried singing the song. I smiled because it really fitted her range. Noela was an unassuming, sweet smiling petite girl you don't think could sing until you see her do.

Our unnamed band, with Noela as front woman, recorded 'Sandalan' at the studio of Vehnee Saturno, the legendary Filipino songwriter. I was with Vehnee inside the studio on the night he was mastering the track. I was seated there watching the prolific tunesmith listen to the track. I was observing how focused he was with the work at hand. That was the takeaway. He wasn't there making me feel he wrote dozens of hit songs and I was too small for his presence. He was making sure I'd be satisfied with the result of a recording crafted in a studio bearing his name.

In the end, the plan to release the song and promote Noela's band went down the drain. The record we did at Saturno Studio was shelved.

Our supposed manager was looking for a particular sound that our band couldn't produce. He didn't like how Arly plays drums. So, the song I wrote out of frustration became extra frustrating when we weren't able to release it. I had to tell my wife the whole thing failed. No new band and record. Noela went to China to be a lounge singer.

Years after shelving 'Sandalan', I started passing it as a demo. I needed a new voice to interpret the song. One night I was covering a band's launch that featured Cooky Chua of 'Color It Red' fame as guest singer. She approached me to say hello and said she owes me a recording. She reminded me that previously when I had met her in another presser many years ago, I had suggested the idea that she record a composition of mine, that is, if she found one good enough. I don't think she ever gave time to listen to anything I submitted. I'm not taking it against her. I understand that she's busy.

There were two other ladies I wrote in my column in *Manila Standard* that I saw fit to record 'Sandalan', but after I emailed them the demo, they never for once replied. I was old enough to understand people and I didn't take such snubs personally.

Anyway, in my continuing search for the appropriate singer for 'Sandalan', I stumbled on a video of one named Angel Andal who joined The Voice Kids Philippines on ABS-CBN. In the video she was singing a version of Mon Del Rosario's 'Sino Ang Baliw' (Who's crazy). It's a song that serves as a good vehicle for singing contest success. The kid really nailed it and I was moved by her performance, along with the millions who viewed it.

As fate would have it, I already met her many months back when I was asked by my bossa nova singing friend Marvin Velasquez to feature her and another young talent in my music column. I messaged her parents and sent them the demo. They responded by sending it back with Angel singing along to it. I felt goosebumps hearing her voice singing 'Sandalan'. Her singing had a certain bite. I won't compare it with that of Noela. They're equally good. It was by grace of God that we didn't procrastinate, and instead moved forward to record the track in January of 2020. If we delayed for a couple of months, we could have missed the chance since Angel won't be allowed to go out in a pandemic-riddled world.

It took just a couple of studio visits for Angel to record her vocals at Forgiven studio owned by music engineer Mark Zoleta who's a believer of my work. At age twelve, she was spectacularly professional. Credit goes to her parents for being very supportive. They're even coaching her how to best perform the track. The kid surely does her homework. Add to the mix Mark whose musical expertise, having been a keyboardist for rocker Lou Bonneivie before he suffered from stroke, helped the song get proper treatment.

For the accompaniment, Arly made a return trip and recorded the drum track. A few years of extra experience turned him into a steadier, more confident drummer. On a separate day it was Eric 'Meng' Villarmino's turn to show his prowess in the guitar department. Here's a musician who became my bandmate when he was just eighteen, recorded a full-length album, went the showband route, played for some celebrity singers, and even played on TV as part of a backing crew for a variety show. I thought he played like how Steve Lukather would play on the track. His lead guitar's dialogue with Angel's bridge vocals is a highlight of the song.

I felt the instrumental part in the initial version was too long, so I put in a new melody line with lyrics, which turned out to fit well with Angel's singing style.

When the song was released in digital format in February of 2020, Angel performed it live during a show at Farmers Plaza in Cubao, Quezon City. That was a new experience for me: hearing my composition debuted by its interpreter in front of the public. It was also among the last face-to-face shows I witnessed as we were just a couple of weeks' away from community lockdown.

Iconic columnist Ricky Lo featured 'Sandalan' in his column in the early days of the quarantined world, while Angel, with me on acoustic guitar, performed the track for *Business Mirror*'s online gig for musical artists.

Near the end of 2020, Noela reconnected with me. He found a manager and they had a studio in Tarlac province. They paid me to cover 'Sandalan' and she and her band recorded it based on the demo we did at Saturno's. Noela's version was released on 17 December.

'Sandalan's' journey is Noela's too. That's why I allowed her to have the track as her debut even if it would directly put her version in competition with Angel's rendition. I can't compare their takes. They're both great. But if forced to give an answer, I'd say Angel is a prodigy, technically gifted songstress that gave 'Sandalan' justice even if she has yet to experience adulting. Noela, on the other hand, possesses the voice of a woman who has gone through hell and back. She makes use of her weapon, tried, and tested, and tired, to say she still can make it through after all.

Both versions were chosen by Spotify editors for inclusion on their platform's New Music Friday, a special playlist for new releases. To be on such a playlist means your record has been deemed worthy of public exposure. The song that my wife inspired found a home in two superb voices.

Inside one of the rooms at Pirate Studios along Sunset Boulevard in Los Angeles, California. Yugel launched his solo recording venture in late 2023, with Ted Reyes (right) of NSFU Publishing as his producer

Chapter 5

Beauty of Harmony

When the eighth Pub Forties digital single came out in May 2021, there was not much expectation because, first, we recorded the track two years ago and have given little attention to it compared with the scheduled-for-release song being recorded on the same sessions: 'Stop the World'. Second, it's Tagalog. Our band is not built for Tagalog lyrics because Aries, for whatever reason, is not comfortable singing songs with Filipino words. He has a tendency to sing it in a way where he sounds like a non-Filipino struggling to speak the language. In short, Aries is better off singing in English.

Thus, when it was apparent that he was not nailing 'Nung Tayo Pa' the way I'd like him to sing it, nor was he getting the melody lines at all since merely pronouncing the words was a struggle, we had no choice but to come up with an alternative plan. He suggested that I sing it myself and instead he'd do a second voice to go with my lead vocal. I'm not the band's lead singer so at first, I wasn't keen on the idea.

Also, the song's narrative was too personal for me, and I felt some pressure. The composition is one I wrote as a closure on my life spent with my ex-girlfriend Mary Ann who subsequently relocated to Italy after we broke up. She got married to an Italian man. I could say I'm happy for her that she ended up with him. I wonder how she could have further put up with a high-maintenance artist-boyfriend. Yeah, me.

The song celebrates the good times by saying, '*Di ko kayang kalimutan ang nangyari sa ating dalawa*' (Can't forget what happened to us two). It is narrating some of our moments in the verses, like '*Pag maglalakad na tayo palayo sa eskuwelahan / Magde-date sa inyo*' (When we're walking away from school and going for a date).

So, there you go, I had to sing the thing I composed in the early 2000s. It was already an old one while we were properly recording it. I did little editing and tried to preserve as much as possible the song as I created it, in particular its bass line that dated back to a demo session in November of 2003. That evening my simple bass adlibbing gave birth to the groove heard right after the exit of the vocals. You may agree that it sounded exciting. That's because I was trying to make the impression that I was enjoying playing the song. In reality, I was addressing a situation as our guitarist that moment wasn't doing its job to play solo. I had to fill that vacuum. Hearing the playback, it sounded good, and I felt lucky it was put on tape. I had to quickly refresh how I played it when it was my time to properly record my bass line—some fifteen years later. I simulated the same feel on the record, and it still excites me hearing it each time.

Aries made good on his vow, and he supplied a sublime vocal harmony that produced that third voice. He made my singing sound better. He also suggested a keyboard part and injected a vocal ploy in the second verse that stressed the idea that we were influenced by Manila Sound. 'Hahahay,' he quipped. Sir Snaffu Rigor, who passed away the year Syato deactivated, would have enjoyed listening to this track for sure!

Aries noted, 'That's the beauty of harmony. When two voices sing in sync, it's as if there are three or four vocals in it.'

On the day it was released, O/C Records, our distributor at the time, obligatorily uploaded its audio clip of the song.

We were kind of surprised that it quickly garnered quite a traction. Other acts would have laughed at how we see the reception as a big boost, but we're a band that virtually had no following, with relatively inactive social media accounts and whose members don't post about our work that much. Even me, I hardly post unless there's something really worth sharing about. That first day, the number of views reached 1,400 with more than a hundred likes. Why be amazed about a small number? A previous release garnered seventy likes in six months!

O/C Records A&R Martin Riggs expressed, 'This is really doing well, guys,' referring to his conclusion that unlike the two previous songs we put out under O/C, this one's really gaining ground.

Having noticed that some people are indeed listening, including one that commented 'underrated bands are the best,' I was expecting 'Nung Tayo Pa' to land the New Music Friday playlist. The song was dropped on Spotify on a Wednesday. By Friday I didn't see it appear on the list. That was a downer, for some hours, temporarily.

Later in the evening I found out that the single was chosen for Fresh Finds Philippines playlist, which caters to indie recordings. The Spotify editors saw the potential of the song in the same way as the others who thumbed up upon hearing it.

Aries joked during a call that I should always sing the Tagalog tracks because it seemed to work. I didn't have to put an underlying meaning to what he said. He was just as happy as I am about the track. I like the good vibes 'Nung Tayo Pa' sent and it has given my voice extra confidence. If Aries and I singing together is a good formula, then so be it.

Vocal recording of Yugel's first single 'Hosanna Kapiling Ka'
in Los Angeles, California. (Photo by Sheryl Reyes)

Chapter 6

Day the Music Dies

'The day the music died,' the defining phrase from the classic *American Pie*, according to its singer-songwriter Don McLean, was an attribute to the crash that killed rock 'n' roll icon Buddy Holly in the late 1950s. Before I learned about that, I thought it was about that hard day's night when John Lennon was assassinated—a brutal moment in the history of music that happened twenty-one years after the plane crash emotionally depicted in the movie *La Bamba*. Yes, the seventeen-year-old behind the classic, Richie Valens, also perished on 'the day the music died'.

The catchphrase already evolved into a nod to a popular musician's death, which in essence is that point when someone's work stops and goes eternal.

A living legend's demise signals the rebirth of his catalogue. I've read that at the time of its release, *Double Fantasy*, Lennon's comeback album after a five-year hiatus to take care of his son Sean, had not exploded as it was hoped, even if it was from an ex-Beatle who self-hibernated. But, in the aftermath of the infamous shooting, the album was quickly appreciated with the heartbreaking realization that the artist behind it won't be able to produce another one. It eventually won the Grammy for Album of the Year, and deservingly so. Lennon's single '(Just Like) Starting

Over' was the perfect lead single for the anticipated return of the rebel Beatle, while 'Woman' became the impassioned posthumous hit, very Lennon in its minimalist chorus, like the one in 'Girl' heard on 'Rubber Soul'. There was 'Watching the Wheels' that served as the poignant backdrop to his house husband period. The album's dark horse, 'I'm Losing You', provided a haunting picture, performed with efficiency, of what may have further come had its singer survived.

In the 1990s, the suicide of Kurt Cobain marked the end of an era and cemented his status as grunge king and symbolical anti-establishment leader of the Gen X youth. The weekend after Michael Jackson died in 2009, his music was celebrated on the streets of America, or so I read.

Chester Bennington's shocking death in 2017 effectively ended the meteoric run of Linkin Park. The band has been in hiatus since. Also, the day Dolores O'Riordan died in a hotel room abruptly disbanded the Cranberries and sealed her place among the few goddesses of rock.

Technically, your music only dies right after your life ceases. Sadly, I personally know people whose music had apparently died long before their time. Most of them are still alive. I still don't know why they quit, though somehow the reasons are quite understandable. I just can't fathom how they had such an option. If talent is a consideration, then I rest my case. More often though, these quitters I have in mind are evidently talented as I had witnessed. Some were even more skilled as I am head-to-head, and obviously more technically gifted than I can ever be.

Sometimes I do ask myself why I chose to be a mainstay. A lot of guys who are more gifted and confident have already given up. I hate to mention names. Back in college I was treated by my rock 'n' roll circle as the sideman, partly because I was in a band with a strong frontman presence. I'm even the third voice in the original Syato line-up, and I have never been acknowledged as a master bass player.

I'd like to believe I had more drive than some of my contemporaries. I can declare that as an advantage because each band I have gotten into, I always end up being the one most determined to get some great results. You may ask every bandmate I got to work with. I think many of them will agree.

I may have mastered the art of facing failure because I can see that some people can't take defeat. It surely affects my mental health seeing my efforts go down the drain without many returns. Yet, once the hurt passes by I'd prepare for the next gig, the next song.

May I insist that whatever you do for music, regardless of if you'd feel miserable about it most of the time, it remains with you and it is part of your body of work. A thing you did fifteen years back would eventually look or sound more special, perhaps be rediscovered and re-evaluated by a new generation of listeners. It happens for real to some artists and it can happen to you.

A failed musician can't give up because making music is a way of life. Yes, you can reinvent yourself, but you can't fool your soul into believing that dropping out is the best way to handle an unfavourable situation. A mate informed me that he's feeling lazy about having to do it the way he used to. He can't pull himself to come into a rehearsal studio with his guitar and do the same thing twice or thrice a week.

Well, life isn't easy for a person with big dreams. That's part of the deal when you are in a band. You have to rehearse over and over to deliver the output via gigs and recording sessions.

Some do declare they're done and ready to smell the roses, even if in essence, you can't retire from music. I've seen a lot of men buying a set of instruments because they're missing their days as a musician. One way or another you get back to your first love, especially when you can already afford it and have some spare time to rock. You should actually give extra time because totally abandoning music is like handing your own child in the care of someone else. You'll regret it while having wine in your big, eerily quiet house.

So, if you're asked when your music will die, you say it can't, unless you allow it to. Our bodies die but not our body of work. If you wonder if it's necessary that your work is recognized by the public, the answer's no. Nobody knows if your music is set to be hailed by people in the next century. An obscure track can one day become famous because someone who isn't born yet will dig your music—something ahead of your time. My generation X was introduced to The Righteous Brothers, a duo from a couple of decades back, after the 1990 movie *Ghost* used 'Unchained Melody' as a theme song.

Your music is your legacy, meant to last beyond your lifetime. People who quit and accept what others think—that they didn't make it—will die as losers. When you have failed that many times, but you know in your heart you've done enough to succeed, that doesn't make you a failure. Why? Because others don't even try.

Chapter 7

Make or Miss

One time during the pandemic lockdown days, I was writing an article about a reality TV show when the idea of submitting a song came to my mind. The press reference material said it is welcoming contributors for its latest edition.

The show, which I wrote about several times on a national paper, is looking for the next big idea. A year ago, just days after the community quarantine was declared and the world descended into a nightmare typical of a Black Mirror episode, The Pub Forties released the song that we recorded during the last two months of a pre-pandemic society. I called it 'Next Big Thing'. It is about my son's passion for the sport of basketball and my belief that his talent and determination would one day make him a star.

I listened back to the track that got included on Spotify's New Music Friday. It felt good. I knew I had to submit. The vibe seemed right. I was on cloud nine due to the recent publication of my first novel *The Lust Regime* (in February 2021) and many of my friends seemed to be genuinely happy that I completed a story of novel length.

The creator of the show is a nice, smart guy who during the show's zoom launch joked that he was obliging his wife to describe him as a creative genius. That was part of his wit.

In my little pitch, I told him that after reflecting on the merits of the show, I thought of offering 'Next Big Thing' as a musical backgrounder to some clips of the upcoming run. His response included his three-word reaction to the track: 'Love the song!' Then he said, 'Let's see how we can use it for the upcoming season.' I followed up by saying that the song's possible exposure would give it a chance to be heard by more people.

In half an hour the good-natured host connected me to the show's production head who created a group chat called, you guess, Next Big Thing. A zoom meeting had been set for the following week to discuss the music, and apparent placement.

You can't blame me for making a big deal on this matter. The show has a fine reputation in the community and the inclusion of my band's song on it could be the break we've been waiting for. I have experienced all sorts of false hopes in the art of lobbying songs. This couldn't be another one, especially with the circumstances that made it likely to happen. Perhaps it helped that I used my pen to promote the show and I had become familiar with the host.

Kaye, upon learning about it, reiterated that 'Next Big Thing' is a good song before anything else. Ryde curiously asked what the song is about after hearing me hum it. I told him the truth: it's about him and the little voice inside him that knows the things he wants to do.

'Next Big Thing' is my ode to Ryde's intense love for the sport that deserves a theme song.

Aries, our band's reliably enthusiastic singer, came up with an extra line he delivered by injecting some world music passage. Because of it we dodged the idea of putting rap in the instrumental part. It gave the song additional spice after its verse, chorus, and bridge. It also showed his high interest for the number.

From time-to-time, Aries puts a line or an instrumental hook that would provide extra bite to an otherwise complete song. Somehow, we couldn't collaborate like I did with Chris and Joseph, but he made up for it through small but significant contributions I'd gladly allow to accommodate. He did it in 'Road Rage' by extending the word 'cab' until the lead guitar takes the ball. In 'Nung Tayo Pa' he suggested a horn line that heightened the disco feel of the number.

It was a pity that his idea of showing scenes of Metro Manila under lockdown interspersed with our shots inside a mock-up design of a musician's pad—designed by 'Design Diva' Joy Delos Reyes whom I wrote about in my column—had only been viewed by a few. We have a damn good song and a tight music video concept capturing the images of a ghostly twenty-first-century pandemic.

This supposed break for 'Next Big Thing' might spell the difference and finally hand the song the popularity it truly deserves.

Alas, everything went down the drain. The production team suddenly stopped communicating and, as far as I know since I did check when it aired, the show came out on TV without our song being heard. I really don't know why it didn't. My heart was too tired to ask.

In showbiz, there's nothing personal when you get dropped or denied. Overthinking about it will not change the fact that it's another setback and I have to live with it. With age I have learned the art of licking my wounds and laughing at things that don't go my way.

What's important is there is a song about my son which I hope will inspire every kid with a dream, especially if one day the tune earns mainstream recognition. There's a line in the song where I say that 'even Simon Cowell sometimes can't tell who among the winners will last'. Everyone has a chance to be the next big thing people will marvel at, talk about, or embrace in their consciousness. But first you have to 'grab the chance' and 'seize the moment when the ball arrives'.

I did when I felt I had to reach out to someone to give my composition, my band's song, the kind of exposure it needs. For the nth time, it did not work. But it shouldn't stop me from going to the next song, next release. We'll only know who or what the next thing will be once it's already that big.

Chapter 8

Shock News

Somehow everything ends on a sad note, especially if we put into the equation life's nature to succumb to death. It's particularly sadder when someone who'd been in the limelight for so long, made countless concert fans and casual listeners delighted, had found himself at the end of a rope.

It's easy to plot the dots as to what caused Jamir Garcia, vocalist of hard rock band Slapshock and the most recognizable Filipino face in that genre, to take his own life. Once I read about him allegedly embezzling money from a bandmate, written by my colleague Poch Concepcion who has a knack for public-revealing internal problems by celebrity musicians, it was obvious he was in trouble.

Something must have gone really wrong in the way the group handled their money. While it's not an unusual dilemma, matters quickly escalated. His band of twenty-three years officially disbanded amid the turmoil that drifted the members in two factions. Based on the news, bassist Lee Nadela, whose brother Renmin I personally know, and guitarist Jerry Basco, his cousin who sued him for estafa and qualified theft, were definitely not on his side.

Nobody expected it would lead to suicide just a month after the disbandment. He hanged himself in his home with a blanket tied to a window. I regularly pass by the hospital where he was brought to, during rides from home to press conferences or meetings. We live in the same area. The police station that reported his cause of death came from Barangay Talipapa where I grew up with my siblings.

It turned out to be a hole Jamir found too deep to get out of. He may have thought of himself going to jail or being maligned endlessly on social media. Sure, he could form a new band with the other members who remained loyal to him, but he obviously feared it would never be the same. None of us, especially himself, thought that a group as solid as theirs could end up in disarray.

Jamir's tragic death is somewhat personal because I knew him, and he was a very nice dude who spoke words with passion and without ever expressing frustration in his voice. You would think that with Slapshock's kind of music, you'd meet an angsty front man with an all-too-familiar attitude that fans couldn't care about as long as they're led to head-banging hysteria during performance proper.

Back in 1999, I attended this concert called 'Rebirth' organized by MTV Pilipinas. It was a gig featuring some of the best bands from the '90s alternative rock scene. To this day it's still one of the most remarkable shows I've seen live. I was a mere college music fan enjoying an all-stars gig along with my brothers. We were willing to wait for all the bands scheduled to perform that night. There were two band set-ups. We could see the Eraserheads setting up on one side while Wolfgang was performing.

Amusingly, fans were shouting for one band name to reiterate that their set is the highlight of the evening. Chants of Slapshock were repeated several times that evening. They just had their breakthrough hit 'Agent Orange'.

They actually came up on stage way past midnight, with many of the fans already too sleepy to stay. We were curious to see them perform and see for myself what the fuss was all about. We held on till the group appeared, and they didn't disappoint. I was sleepy myself, but my heart was racing watching them. Agent Orange was urging me to 'get up, get up, get up'.

In my journey as a journalist specializing in music, hands down Jamir was among my nicest interviewees. He was not particularly witty nor profound, but he spoke with sincerity. I would believe in things he said because he was not trying to be cool, only stating things as unadorned facts. In an article I wrote for *The Philippine Star*—which stressed on his band's sixteen years—at the time, about commitment to the profession, I quoted him as saying, 'I had no plan B. *Nung nagbanda kami wala kaming* fallback at never *ako nagka*-option to do other things. *Kaya nagpa*-tattoo *ako ng husto*' (When we formed the band we didn't think of a fallback. It was never my option to do other things, so we had ourselves tattooed). The tattoos meant he never wanted to go back to corporate work. He was once a mechanic in a car company.

In his case, there's really no point in going back to such a state considering that corporate sponsors themselves had well provided for Slapshock. Their endorsement of the Dickies apparel allowed me to chat with them on a number of occasions. Publicist and showbiz reporter Gorgy Rula would invite me to do interviews with the band. Jamir had become used to me talking to them. In the last interview I did, in their gig along Roxas Boulevard, Manila in the summer of 2019, he said something I would cherish forever. He noted he was seeing my Facebook posts of my kid Ryde playing basketball. He said, *'Ang galing ng anak mo sa basketball'* (Your kid's great at basketball). Apparently, he was into the sport and could recognize a talent.

I did plan to bring along my kid in a future interview so they could see each other in person. But as often the case for plans that can no longer happen whatever you do, death interfered.

It's not foolish to say that Jamir's death on 26 November 2020 was hastened by the pandemic that took away a lot in the year it unleashed its diabolical force. Musicians lost gigs, earnings, and hope. Optimistic people said that 2020, too, shall pass. Sadly, a lot of beautiful lives did pass during one dreadful year.

California, US: The author with his mother Amalia who,
along with his late father Eulogio Sr., has always supported
his passion for music and writing

Chapter 9

Navigating a Pandemic

Our band was embarking on an exciting phase when the pandemic stalled everything. We were already hanging out and in principle had convinced Bong Baluyot, the manager who put Orange & Lemons on the Philippine band scene map, to handle us. He has become a friend as I walked on the path of rock journalists.

On March 6, 2020, Eric Villarmino, whom we called Meng during Syato days, jammed with us for the purpose of formally joining the group. As expected, he passed it. We were eyeing for the next rehearsals when in a few days' time, the Covid-19 pandemic period officially started, punctuated by a lockdown that wouldn't allow us to see each other for two years.

We pushed on with the release of 'Next Big Thing', the latest song we tackled. Who knew that the next big one would turn out to be a virus that would kill millions and scare the world over?

We released two more songs, and an EP of demo takes, under lockdown where we the members communicated through audio and video calls. All the tracks on *DocumentAries*, as we called it obviously as a play on Aries' name, were either unreleased recordings, or songs treated in the studio to make them releasable.

In late April of 2022, the four of us—Aries Espinosa, Vince Borromeo, James Casas, and I—were able to gather back ourselves in the same room. The idea of having Eric into the fold was dropped. We thought the closeness among us four makes us the band's classic line-up, with all due respect to everyone who came in and went along the way, including Eric, of course.

May Manuel, the lady who in 2019 watched us play and said she's convinced we're that good and authentic, and her singing musician boyfriend Andrew, joined our jams at Vince's new office. We used to regularly jam at the Borromeo family's previous law office along Scout Alcaraz in Quezon City. It was our escape from regular routines; hence, we joked about calling a future album or EP *Escape to Alcaraz*, not from Alcatraz. It is where we make music together.

That set of songs could only be an EP of six tracks as completed. The journey to crafting them was a fun ride, among the best of our days playing for and with each other. We felt we were more intact creatively.

We started off with a song I thought deeply about at the peak of the pandemic scare. It's called 'Departure Area'. It has nothing to do with the exit of people from this worldly universe and into the great beyond. The title-phrase refers to a boring spot. Somehow it synced with the Alcaraz escape idea.

Years ago, I was waiting at the departure area of NAIA (Ninoy Aquino International Airport) for a flight to Albay to meet a notable political figure who invited a pool of media representatives from Manila. I was feeling bored and so I started coming up with a tune and a set of words. I saw a pretty lady seated somewhere. I was sure we'd be on the same flight. So, I imagined myself asking her '*Naboboring ka na ba sa* departure area? *Sasamahan kitang lumipad*' (Are you feeling bored in this departure area? Let me fly with you). The Filipino/Tagalog line became the lyric hook of a new song. With Vince somehow taking the lead with his quirky ideas, the track developed into a theatrical piece mixing various musical influences and out-of-the-box lyric writing. Vince contributed a Visayan verse. Aries injected Bruce Willis in the opening verse.

Then I filled up the bridge with a list of classic Filipino movies, thirty in total.

I recently bought a keyboard with keys suitable for my heavy hand and it proved useful to our first physical meetup dusting off the rust. I wrote a melody around four chords, Am-F-C-E, which according to a YouTube clip I saw could be jumbled in various combinations to compose several, separate songs. The intro riff I came up with gave birth to 'One Good Soul', with its serious mood capturing how I felt about Anne Frank's belief that despite what was going on in the concentration camp where she was after her family was captured and imprisoned by the Nazis, people are 'truly good at heart'. In my composition, I want to express the nobility of saving that one good person perhaps stranded among a pack of meanies. I let Aries write most of the words, as we had done in another composition off my head in the middle of the lockdown months.

That one is called 'Cutting Shards'. Its melody must have been influenced by the music of Gin Blossoms, which I'm a fan of.

It was raining hard one Friday and the tune came out easily. Except for one line, 'Someday I'll find my way back to your heart', I found it hard to find the rest of the words, so I called Aries. Later when we rehearsed the song as a foursome, Vince came up with a bass line simply sounding haunting not to include on the master track. I realized it was not easy for me to play it, but I went through it anyway. We're really locking in as a group; it's a disservice not to endure the difficulty of putting in a good riff.

Aries was obviously inspired by how we have gelled as a band that he came up with a damn good composition himself. 'Hakbang Ka Lang' (Just step in), with its retro dance vibe perfectly fits his voice and character. I happily contributed a bass line that I think gave justice to such a vibe.

Thanks to May for always trusting my capability as a composer. She pushed for 'Kay Sarap' (Oh It's Good), a piece

I wrote in the late '90s, to be our bounce back recording after two years of remote relationship. The song's lyrics harked back to my youth, and she sees it as a fitting reunion song for friends, relatives, and ex-lovers who have not seen each other due to the pandemic. Andrew's arrangement that turns it into a hybrid of old and new, proved crucial when we recorded it. We had a template that really worked!

Hearing the finished product of the EP *Escape to Alcaraz*, which is definitely an improvement from the one of out-takes and original song demos, it didn't feel like we were rushing when we were doing it. I had to squeeze in some of the studio recording hours before I punch in for duty at *CNN Philippines* where I was working at the time. Often, I'd find myself tired by the third hour. Either my workload was taking its toll on me, or it was an indication of me already aging and my stamina for the recording routine not being as strong as it had been. As long as good music is delivered, such matter is not much of an issue.

Before I took a break to see my mother and America, we had this one last jam at Vince's place, and we decided to record vocals for a song he wrote called 'Titos Your Amigos'. He had long proposed for this track to be recorded and as it turned out it was fun delivering our vocals, all four of us, each trying to give advice to the young in wacky voices of various pitches and characters.

Nearly six years after The Pub Forties started, we recorded a relatively low output of eighteen tracks, a small catalogue but which I am proud of big-time. I want the public at large to eventually discover our music not primarily because it's ours but that some listeners may be touched by it in positive ways.

Our recordings out of lockdown prove that a band of brothers can survive a pandemic, lick wounds, and get back together, recuperating and soldiering on.

Chapter 10

Right Choice

I'm connected with some members of the media as I am one myself. For that, it's not far-fetched for me to get featured from time to time either as part of a band or the songwriter behind a newly released song.

However, to be on the music page of a national broadsheet in a solo feature, on a premier space, was quite something. *Business Mirror* came out with a full-page feature of me on a Sunday, April 25, 2021, with the title 'Re-introducing Yugel Losorata', and the sub-head 'Music and letters are in the blood'. The page is *Soundstrip*, which publishes stories related to musicians.

Becoming a novelist gave me extra merit as a subject, along with the help of a couple of friends in the biz. Columnist Tony Maghirang suggested that he'd write about me after I gave him a signed copy of my novel. His offer was one I couldn't refuse. It pays to choose the right friends, I guess. He and editor Edwin Sallan, who's also a long-time pal, connived in giving me a feature of a lifetime, or hopefully, the first of many of such magnitude. They were both pioneers of music writing in the country; two men who wrote for the *Jingle* magazine and are still writing as of 2024.

An article focused on highlighting the fact that I've embraced both music-making and book-writing is a validation that my efforts to empower art in the way I understand meant something to a couple of legitimate journalists. Yes, they are my friends. But they could tell me to my face what's newsworthy and deserving of newspaper space.

If I am to analyse in a weird way, my evolution as writer-musician is brought about by my failed attempts to establish myself either as a celebrated writer or a rock star. I never made it to UST's campus paper *The Varsitarian* when I was in the university, nor even to *Flames*, our college paper in AB (Bachelor of Arts). Further back, I didn't get featured on the high school paper *Young Achievers*. I wasn't a young achiever, save for some honourable mentions—'Best in Deportment' medals, and a 'Most Diligent' citation by my amiable third grade class adviser Mr Mar Arabit.

The Dreamers' failure to get a record contract was a bitter taste that haunted me for long. It is one of the reasons why I badly wanted to get signed at all costs. It's never about putting one over Chris Datijan, my teenage songwriting partner, but to address that frustration without having to reform our group.

I welcomed the new millennium feeling like a big loser with so much to prove. Such a mentality may have helped me in a way. But what does being successful actually mean anyway? Success is relative, they say. I know people who have not recorded a thing but are happy doing cover songs and getting hefty tips from paying bar patrons.

At first, I wondered why some people I know who used to have their bylines had stopped writing after some setback. People change careers after failing at something. Others concentrate on whatever that pays the bill or gives them a more relaxing routine. That makes sense.

If we ask the common man for his definition of a successful person, you bet the answer would be one with lots of money or has a corporate title, which also equates to having money. It's basic for a man who only sees the surface. Not everyone can make it to the hit parade. Not everyone is the next JK Rowling.

I believe that being successful is finding that thing you want to do and doing everything to be good at it. It may not be a guarantee that you'll enjoy lots of money with it. But at least you made the right choice and you're not living a lie. Money and recognition eventually follow, sometimes it will after death.

If you believe in something, there's really no alternative nor shortcuts. I cannot force people to listen to songs I composed nor pull them to read articles with my byline, or books I authored. Likewise, I cannot be stopped from doing them. For me, that's throwing away my purpose for living.

If I opt for other careers, well-paying I suppose, I can end up in a well-furnished office with a thin-waisted secretary helping me handle paper works. But I won't be as happy as I should be.

To be fair, working in a media outfit is different from being in a regular corporate office. Reporters, editors, writers, and photojournalists behave much differently from employees who have to present reports or meet in a boardroom to exchange jargons or acronyms only they could understand. There's a certain feel in being a member of the fourth estate, which I find empowering and fun.

Even while sensing that being in the media in the Philippines is not a high-paying career, and leading the musician's life is much less compensatory financially, I knew what I had to do. I have to keep my byline and continue making music. There are other ways to earn to augment the need for income. What's the use of having a network of media professionals or being part of the music scene if I can't use them to get some other gigs!

Accepting that you have failed in your early tries should make you ready to face an even tougher road ahead. Don't worry because the past failures made you wiser enough to face the music and make it better.

The author having coffee after watching a Beatles-themed musical in Southern California, November 2022

Chapter 11

Gently Breaking News

It was a Friday afternoon, year 2022. I was a few minutes early to my shift as senior copy editor for *CNN Philippines*, a news channel carrying the highly reputable international brand, which hired me in the midst of an ongoing Covid-19 pandemic.

I greeted the security guard at the reception and signed the logbook that made it official I was on duty. As I walked to my station where I would edit news scripts and digital articles for the next eight hours, something beautiful caught my attention. It was actually not something, but someone.

There in a corner, standing in utmost confidence, talking to somebody in her gorgeous get up and figure, with her finely combed hair, and neatly worn dress, was one of the lady anchors. Either she's done with her newscast assignment or just about to fill in for someone.

Whatever her schedule that day was really not my concern. At that moment I was trying to decide whether to approach her or not, strike up a small talk or even tell her that when I was young, it was my dream to have an anchorwoman for a girlfriend.

Ultimately, I did not. I just let her slip away and I went on to do my work for the day. I never really got to address my shyness with women, especially with ladies who make my heart palpitate in a swoop. That is among the reasons why I became a writer, and a songwriter. I can't manage to say things verbally. I have to jot them down.

My stint with *CNN Philippines*, though short, was sweet in a number of ways. One, the job forced me to come out of the house after two years, and in doing so I conquered my fear of contracting the virus again.

Two, I've gone around the print media circuit as a writer for quite a while, with my byline having appeared in several national broadsheets and online sites. Serving for a broadcast news channel was a breath of fresh air, must I say, an icing on the cake so to speak to my run as journalist in the Philippines.

Three, I got to further hone my skill as writer-editor considering it's a lot different breaking news on TV than through published articles. I felt happy when I passed the exam during the application process because in a way it legitimized once and for all my being a journalist.

And four, while I've met broadcast news professionals in media circles, it was never on a day-to-day basis that I got to be with them. My work routine in *CNN Philippines* allowed me to observe how the anchors, with the help of their hard-working teams, do it, and how they are off screen.

Back in 1986, I was a youngster curiously watching the EDSA People Power Revolution unfold on TV. A group of anti-dictatorship journalists were broadcasting what was happening and I noticed two ladies, June Keithley and Maan Hontiveros, bravely putting themselves in the spotlight—going against a regime being publicly accused of many crimes, including press freedom.

From that point on I've always been fascinated by what a lady journalist can and does. In college my friends would vocally express their liking towards the hottest starlets of the day. I would quietly tell myself that I prefer the smart, intelligent, and beautifully classy news presenter gently breaking news.

I married Kaye Villagomez partly because she's a journalist, who at the time we met was writing about the entertainment scene in a no-nonsense way and with aplomb. She's a voluptuous lady who's in control and is hardly ever rattled amid the pressure at hand. She had become my life's anchor and my woman. That's poetic license from a hopeless romantic.

At *CNN Philippines*, I was given a full view, from the control room, and around the newsroom, of seeing a certain kind of woman resembling my wife and who makes the art of telling the news extra wonderful to the ear, to the eyes, and to the pen of a songwriter.

I was definitely okay to stay and serve the brand longer. But fate intervened and I had to fly to the United States to visit my mother who was still grieving over my father's death.

Before I even thought about returning to my post, which my boss said I could go back to anytime, the network, sadly, had to be shut after a good nine-year run. By February 2024, *CNN Philippines* was no more.

I only have a couple of memorabilia items as souvenirs from the company. But I got enough inspiration for a song, or maybe more. A few days after I landed in America, I started writing a tune, my first attempt at songwriting after a fifteen-hour flight from Manila to Los Angeles, which I wanted to call 'Anchorwoman'. It is a title already fleshed out in full regalia back in the newsroom.

Naturally I just had to revert back to writing for newspapers and online, my comfort zone. My byline would always pop up from time to time and I don't see myself telling friends that this is my last article; or in the case of my musicianship, my last composition. The writing of words and composing of melodies shall continue until I write thirty. In my book, writers and musicians don't retire.

Coda

When I reconnected with Ted Reyes whom I first met as front man of The Free Souls and whose songwriting style greatly influenced that of mine, I was seeing an old friend who decided to relocate to Los Angeles after living in New York for two decades. I happened to be staying in Southern California and I was just a train ride away from him. Our meet-up led him to verbally offer me a recording deal that will make him produce my new compositions into proper records, and then release them under NSFU (New Sounds from Underground) Publishing, which he put up essentially as a label for his music and other Fil-Americans. It was a big break as it opened the door for me to become, albeit reluctantly, as a solo artist named simply Yugel.

Around that time, I had written a Christmas love song as I long to be with my wife, and our son. It's a piano ballad that Ted turned into a layered recording, with him backing up my lead vocals in the chorus and other key parts of this relatively short song, with a busy chord run I'm quite proud of. Being with my mother after my father passed away physically separated me from my own family for a while. I took some refuge in songwriting, as I always do in times of anxiety and uncertainty. There has to be some music wherever you are in the world, struggling for and with it, because life without music is death.

Ted called out my name as I was looking for him at the parking lot in front of Gerry's Grill in Artesia, southeast of Los Angeles County in California, his voice felt like that of a long-lost cousin you once played syato (the street game) with in a remote province in the Philippines. He used to be part of my youth, a key figure in those heady days when a gig spot at Mayric's bar along España, Manila, meant like you're on your way to making it big in the music scene. The Dreamers were friends and fans of The Freesouls. To see him in person after a long while was like a salute to my youth and a wink to a future of possibilities.

It still haunts me to this day thinking that The Freesouls were somewhat robbed of the fame they deserved after their follow-up single to 'Shindig' was banned on radio stations. Some unreasonable executives thought that their supposedly wholesome song 'Yatehan' is an explicit euphemism for sex.

In my mind, the triumph of Ted's group would make the road for my band less rough. For one he was already friends with some industry people, and he could guide us had he stayed in the Philippines. We lost contact. I could feel some momentum was lost.

It may not be a coincidence that in the same year he flew out of the Philippines to relocate to New York, The Dreamers disbanded as well. If I could turn back the clock it was best that we pushed on. Let me just say that the mood of the times, at least within our circle, forced us to quit with a heavy heart.

Modesty aside, Syato somehow replicated the level of success The Freesouls had. Both bands got signed by a mainstream label, were launched on Sunday noon TV, enjoyed radio airplays for a couple of singles off their debut albums, and then cut short their runs. Ted formed a couple of new groups, Bleud and The Happy Analogues, as a Fil-Am. The revamped Syato personnel was basically a new band, and years later I went on to form The Pub Forties.

Ted moved to Los Angeles in the spring of 2023. I flew in from Manila in the fall of 2022, landing at the Los Angeles

Airport on a Sunday morning to be with my mother who's still grieving the death of my father. Fate made it happen for us to get reacquainted and give our friendship a second wave.

Seeing an old friend, someone who saw you when you were just a penniless boy trying to figure out what to do when school is over, could open new doors that you never thought were accessible. Old friends are like your brothers. It really doesn't matter how long you've not communicated with each other. They'd help without expecting something in return. I felt that when Ted offered to produce a composition I wrote and which he also asked me to sing myself.

So, on another Sunday, I was inside one of the rooms at Pirate Studios, right on the famous Sunset Boulevard in LA. It felt surreal being there to record vocals for 'Hosanna Kapiling Ka', one of the songs I had written while spending my first months in the US. I bumped into some young, movie-star handsome American musician with all the gears. Ted was there with Sheryl, his long-time soulmate, his Yoko Ono. We were in Studio 8 and the set-up was new to me. There was no mixing engineer you never met dealing with a track I wrote and suggesting some tweaks I wouldn't even consider. Ted is a hands-on producer whose instincts I trust so there was his laptop and Hofner bass, which he brought for me to play with. It was a dream moment. Ted, for all his songwriting and recording exploits, was producing me and giving praises when I was singing the song right!

Why would someone who'd been to various bands suddenly go solo? I asked for Ted's advice who himself had launched a solo career, even putting out his own take to his biggest hit-to-date 'Bye Bye Na', originally sung by rocker Rico Blanco for a songwriting competition where the entry was a finalist. I could have naturally used the name Syato even if I'm the only one on board. Perhaps it was okay to ask my mates in The Pub Forties to give me the blessing to release my song as our latest single.

Yet, everything pointed to a move that was not part of my plan. Go solo. Release songs as an artist named Yugel. Drop the often-misspelled Losorata.

Well, it dawned on me that here's the thing. If it's not your plan, then it is God's plan. When I accepted what my inner voice was telling me, it was easy to say yes. Ted's offer was friendly too. He'll get a cut from the recording material he produces, if and when it earns and I still got my song rights, meaning I have the freedom to record the same composition however I want without having to worry about contract details. We can work on songs as long as I have compositions I want recorded. Exciting days ahead, back at Sunset Boulevard or wherever we end up recording.

It's valuable for every musician to have good control of their songs. I've heard countless stories of Filipino songwriters crying out loud after learning that they don't have a hold to their songs. They can't do what they want to a composition they so cherished about without consulting the record label that owns its publishing rights. Whether or not it is the fault of some songwriters for not reading what's in the contract before signing, fact remains there's something in there that is not favourable for artists, or their mental health.

My mentality is to never call it quits being a musician with or without a band. I really don't have a choice but to continue making music wherever I am, and as much as my age and ability can. So, two days before I turned forty-six, 'Hosanna Kapiling Ka' appeared on digital platforms. I informed friends that it's a new venture for me and I have to start somewhere.

I grew up hearing or being told that doing music is not a viable means to have regular earnings. Not everyone can turn their musicianship for bread and butter. Being in a band is a pastime to most people who believe it's just a passing phase in their lives. You should be engaged in a real job, and if there's extra time, make use of your artistic talent while outside of the eight-hour daily shift.

That's correct, and it largely has to do with the prevailing vibe of the place you're in.

Fortunately for me, I have been blessed enough to have my writing skill as a fallback. My life as a journalist has served me well in providing that balance that kept my feet planted as a person with a byline and an artist with some songs written in the hope of getting them recorded.

I saw it myself, how music can be that frustrating as a profession. You can end up crafting good songs that nobody listens to. People will make you feel irrelevant. You'd feel ashamed that very few know your band, or a person you think is your fan would suddenly express their thoughts about how you can improve your act.

It's all part of the struggles that are there to break your spirit. The question is, should it break you? The answer is definitely no. You being a musician is an essential part of your being. You make music because there is something to express, and you have the outlet.

It's wrong to associate your passion for music with irresponsibility and childishness. Being in a band can sadly be the route to engaging in too much drinking, taking drugs, or having illicit sex only if you allow it. The art of making music is never at fault. It's how you treat your art that will determine how that thing you love and do will turn your life around. It's not all about money, nor hits, fame, and bragging rights. It's how music is keeping your soul intact, making you feel bliss, allowing you to inspire others, and turning your struggles into some form of a good story, call it success if you may, by, say, writing a book about it.

Acknowledgements

I'm grateful to all the good people whose names I mentioned in this book. This would not be made whole without you being present in or passing by my life.

Thank you especially to my mother, Amalia Losorata, for being consistently caring as she always is, giving me a cup of coffee or preparing a hearty meal as I was completing and editing my essay entries in her home in the beautiful state of California.

To the Deita family, my elder sister Amelia, brother-in-law kuya Steve, nephew Angelo, and niece Ammilyn, as well as my youngest sister Karen, for serving as my proper guide in navigating the United States. The renewed hope I've been feeling since seeing America for the first time, enjoying its weather, vast landscapes, and the company of its people, made the completion of this book more fun.

To my wife, Kaye, the girl who makes me laugh, for being the one constant companion sharing my ups and downs as a recording artist and music journalist.

To the EL (Eulogio Losorata) Clan, the Villagomez and Dela Ysla families for their unconditional support.

To Rosabella Jao-Arribas and Ted Reyes for the value they give on my writing and friendship, and for reaching out to help me lighten my path to a future of opportunities and sweet dreams.

To Cerdan Smith, the American Dream believer from Los Angeles, who sees my worth and potential.

To Atty Pia Lewis who firmly believes that I am extraordinary, and to others both in the Philippines and the US who share the same belief.

Let me enumerate some record labels that have helped me in my musical journey one way or another: Ivory Music & Video / Soundscape Publishing / Enterphil, Candid Records, MCA Music, Warner Music Philippines, Neptune Publishing, O/C Records, Widescope Entertainment, Curve Entertainment, GMA Records, and Polyeast Records. Likewise, the media outlets where my byline has appeared: *Manila Bulletin*, *The Philippine Star*, *Yahoo Philippines* (Southeast Asia), *PEP.ph*, *Manila Times*, *Business Mirror*, and *Manila Standard* where I have been writing a column since 2018.

I need not thank people who deprived me of a break, ignored me for whatever reason, and somehow belittled me at some instance. But since they're part of my journey that is continuing for all the right reasons, I can't discount their significance in the plot. Every sweet sensation is made sweeter with a bitter aftertaste.